WILLIAMS-SONOMA

MASTERING

Cakes
Fillings & Frostings

Author
ELINOR KLIVANS

General Editor
CHUCK WILLIAMS

Photographer
BILL BETTENCOURT

fP
FREE PRESS

NEW YORK · LONDON · TORONTO · SYDNEY

Contents

About this book

Mastering Cakes, Fillings & Frostings offers every reader a cooking class in book form, a one-on-one lesson with a seasoned teacher standing by your side, explaining each recipe step-by-step—with plenty of photographs to illustrate every detail.

Birthday cakes, holiday cakes, afternoon-snack cakes—everyone knows that cakes are among the most versatile and most appreciated of all desserts. But too many of us are afraid that if we try to make a cake, we'll be disappointed with the result. This book dispels that fear. Here, you'll discover a wealth of cake recipes with clear instructive text and photographs that will make even the first-time cake baker confident from the moment the flour goes into the bowl.

Here's how this book comprises a complete introductory course on cakes, fillings, and frostings: It begins with descriptions of the different kinds of cakes you will be making, along with guidelines on mixing and baking batters, information on ingredients, and ideas for serving. Next comes the Basic Recipes chapter, which includes popular frostings, fillings, and decorative elements, all of them essential cake-making building blocks. This is followed by an illustrated techniques chapter that will teach you eighteen key skills, from how to separate an egg to how to whip cream to how to fill and frost a layer cake. The Simple Cakes chapter provides instructions for several easy-to-make favorites, including carrot cake, angel food cake, and pound cake. In Cake Layers & Sheet Cakes, you are carefully guided through the steps to make the classic sponge cakes and butter cakes that are the foundation of any cake baker's repertoire. Finally, all your newly mastered knowledge is put to work when you turn to the recipes in Special Occasion Cakes.

With *Mastering Cakes, Fillings & Frostings* beside you, you'll soon be baking cakes for every occasion with ease.

Working with the Recipes

Nothing is more of a crowd-pleaser than the appearance of a beautiful cake. But to make any cake, you must first learn some basic techniques. You need to know how to prepare and mix ingredients for the batter, how to bake it, and finally how to decorate the cake. As you begin to make the cakes in these pages, think of this book as your very own cooking teacher, guiding you at every step along the way.

Learning to make cakes, as with most newly acquired skills, requires practice. This book will help you gain the confidence, through practice, to bake a variety of cakes with ease. First, you will learn basic recipes that will teach you how to make a variety of fillings, frostings, and decorations.

Each subsequent recipe chapter begins with at least two master recipes, which lead you step-by-step, with both pictures and words, through a classic cake recipe. Tackle these key skill-building recipes

first. Their easy-to-follow instructions will make you feel as if a cooking teacher is there to help you along the way.

Once you've worked through the master recipes, you'll be ready to try some of the other recipes in each chapter. Secure in the skills you've already developed, your confidence as a baker will grow as you make these slightly more challenging cakes.

This book not only provides a comprehensive curriculum for baking cakes, but also offers a multitude of

ways to practice your newly acquired abilities. For example, once you've mastered a classic angel food cake, you'll be ready to tackle a chiffon cake drizzled with a tangy orange glaze. You can also practice by making the variations that accompany many of the recipes. Soon you will be eager—and able—to assemble many multilayered cakes with fillings, frostings, and decorations.

For tips about how to stock your kitchen with basic cake-making tools and equipment, turn to pages 132–35.

Types of Cakes

Cakes vary widely in flavor, density, and difficulty. Bakers divide them into two main types: butter cakes, which rely on chemical leaveners for their loft, and foam cakes, which are leavened with beaten eggs and call for little or no fat. But cakes can also be categorized according to how easy or difficult they are to make, which is how the recipes are arranged in this book. You will begin with the easiest cakes and graduate to more challenging ones.

Simple Cakes

These cakes share two common characteristics: they are easy to make and they keep well. This chapter starts with Pound Cake (page 49), which is particularly dense and fine crumbed and can be flavored in a variety of ways. Both Apple Cake (page 63) and Carrot Cake (page 70) call for oil, rather than butter, making them especially easy to mix. For Pineapple Upside-Down Cake (page 67), a simple yellow-cake batter is poured over precisely arranged fruit, baked, and then inverted to serve. The Orange Chiffon Cake (page 74) carries with it distinguishing traits of a foam cake and a butter cake. In contrast, Angel Food Cake (page 57) is a classic foam cake that contains no fat.

Moist bite-sized cakes based on brown butter and hazelnuts (filberts) can be baked in 45 minutes, while a fudgelike flourless cake gets its inimitable flavor from the best chocolate you can buy.

Sheet and Layer Cakes

Here, you'll find one of the best-known foam cakes, the light, airy sponge cake, in both vanilla and chocolate versions. You'll also discover the génoise, which blends elements of both foam cakes and butter cakes, and two popular butter cakes, a classic yellow cake and a chocolaty devil's food.

Special Occasion Cakes

These beautiful cakes, rich with frosting or glaze, buttercream or pastry cream, lemon curd or ganache, are luscious confections for special occasions. Although many of them take time to make, they are worth every minute of your labor. Among them is a stately birthday cake of sponge cake layers brushed with vanilla syrup, filled with chocolate buttercream, and then covered in chocolate frosting, and the celebratory yule log–shaped Bûche de Noël, a rolled chocolate sponge cake concealing chocolate buttercream and topped with chocolate curls.

Despite its name, Boston Cream Pie is not a pie at all, but instead layers of tender-crumbed yellow cake filled with pastry cream and topped with a thick chocolate glaze.

Custardlike cheesecakes are in a class all their own. Satiny and rich, they are built on cheese, typically cream cheese or ricotta, and baked with either a crumb crust or no crust. Finally, individual chocolate cakes are remarkably easy to make and they can be baked in less than 20 minutes, they won't wait for guests—their centers must still be warm and soft when the cakes are eaten.

Ingredients for Cakes, Fillings & Frostings

Here you'll find general descriptions of all the basic ingredients used in this book. Some of them you'll buy only when you need them, such as cream cheese and buttermilk. Others you'll want to keep on hand, including all-purpose and cake flours, baking soda and baking powder, granulated and confectioners' sugars, large eggs, unsalted butter, unsweetened and semisweet chocolates, and vanilla extract—a well-stocked pantry for making cakes.

Dry Ingredients

Most cake making relies on two types of wheat flour, all-purpose (plain) flour and cake (soft-wheat) flour. Unbleached all-purpose flour has a slight ivory cast and a better flavor than the bleached version, which has been chemically treated. It is well suited to more dense-textured cakes, such as Pound Cake (page 49). Cake flour is whiter, due to bleaching, than all-purpose flour. It is best for lighter cakes with a more tender crumb, such as Angel Food Cake (page 57).

Granulated sugar, the most commonly used type of sugar, is made up of small white crystals. Confectioners' (icing) sugar, which is a powdered form of granulated sugar, is usually blended with a little cornstarch (cornflour) to prevent caking. Brown sugar gets its color from molasses and comes in golden and dark brown varieties. Different sugars behave differently, so be sure to use the type specified in the recipe.

Baking powder and baking soda (bicarbonate of soda) are both white powders. Be sure that you reach for the right one when assembling ingredients.

Regular table salt is fine to use for the recipes in this book. It is usually fine-grained and contains additives to help keep it from caking. Coarser kosher salt or fine sea salt can be substituted.

Wet Ingredients

Grade A large eggs were used to test the recipes in this book. Larger or smaller eggs won't yield the same results. If you're using a recipe in which egg whites

remain raw, and you're concerned about safety, use pasteurized egg whites, which are packaged in easy-pour containers and stocked in the supermarket cold case. If you're whipping them into stiff peaks, they will take a little longer to beat than fresh egg whites.

Whole milk has a higher fat content and is generally thicker than low-fat or nonfat milk. Buttermilk is thicker than milk and has a creamier texture and a tangy flavor. Sometimes it also has tiny specks of butter in it. Nonfat or low-fat buttermilk can be used. Heavy cream, also known as double cream or whipping cream, has an ivory color and a higher fat content than milk and buttermilk.

Cream cheese, often sold in blocks, and sour cream, which is softer, are sold in a variety of fat contents. For the best flavor, use the full-fat versions of both.

Always use unsalted butter, rather than salted, when baking. It is fresher and allows you to control the amount of salt in a recipe. European-style butter, which is becoming more available, lends fuller flavor to baked goods.

Flavorings

Fruits, nuts, and spices provide flavor and can also be used as an attractive garnish or decoration. Purchase fruits only when they are in season. Buy the freshest spices and nuts that you can find in a store with a high turnover.

When purchasing extracts (essences), such as vanilla or almond, be sure the labels indicate they are pure. Never purchase an imitation extract.

Almond paste is available in cans or sealed plastic tubes that keep it fresh and moist. Be sure to buy almond paste,

rather than marzipan, which contains a higher percentage of sugar.

Liqueurs, such as Grand Marnier, should be added only in small amounts, as they are intensely flavored.

Like liqueurs, instant coffee powder, which can now easily be found in most supermarkets, is needed only in small amounts. It will dissolve into any liquid, adding a coffee flavor.

Chocolate

Always buy the best chocolate you can afford and be sure to use the type of chocolate specified in a recipe, as any substitutions will change the recipe's sugar and fat content, and flavor.

Cocoa powder is sold in two types: regular and Dutch process (which is treated with an alkali solution). The latter is used for the recipes in this book.

Understanding Baking Ingredients

Here you'll find more detailed descriptions of all the basic ingredients in this book. Each ingredient is categorized according to how it functions in the recipe—whether it is responsible for structure, texture, leavening, flavoring, or a combination. You'll learn that many ingredients can have dual purposes. For example, butter can play a role in flavor, and it will also give your cake a tender texture.

Structural Ingredients

The structure of most cakes is primarily due to the addition of two protein-rich ingredients, flour and eggs.

The proteins present in flour contribute to the formation of gluten, a critical structure-building element. However, cake batters, unlike most bread doughs, are stirred rather than kneaded, so that these flour-based proteins do not develop the same strong, elastic network of gluten strands found in bread doughs. If they did, your cakes would bake up tough and chewy.

Some gluten formation is necessary, of course, to ensure that your cakes rise nicely in the heat of the oven. Because different flours have different protein contents, the type you use will help determine your cake's final structure. For example, all-purpose (plain) flour has a relatively high protein content (although not as high as bread flour), which results in more gluten and a rather sturdy structure, as in the Pound Cake on page 49. A flour with a low protein content, and thus less gluten-producing power, such as cake (soft-wheat) flour, yields a lighter, airier structure, as in the Vanilla Sponge Cake on page 81.

The proteins in eggs play a somewhat different role in a cake's structure. When they are heated, their proteins coagulate and become rigid, which is key in holding a batter together and creating a light and tender structure. When eggs are stirred over direct heat, as when making Citrus Curd (page 26), the agitation from constant stirring keeps the protein strands short, preventing a solid network from forming and producing a smooth, spoonable consistency.

Textural Ingredients

A cake's texture can range from dense and firm to light and airy. A number of everyday ingredients are responsible for these differences.

Liquids, such as milk or buttermilk, contribute to a moist and tender texture. So does sugar, which readily absorbs liquid, depriving flour proteins of what they need to form gluten. This rivalry for limited resources helps keep a cake's texture soft and light during baking.

Whole eggs, which have a high water and fat content, add moisture as well. They also help to distribute air throughout a batter, to ensure a uniform texture. Egg yolks alone are a good source of fat, which they disperse evenly, contributing to a tender crumb.

Fats such as butter and oil are known as shortening agents because they help shorten gluten strands. This action keeps the cake stable as it bakes and prevents a tough crumb from developing. Such fats also coat individual flour particles, which short-circuits gluten formation as well.

Chemical Leavening

Chemical leaveners activate a chemical reaction in which gas is generated, giving cake batter height as it bakes.

Baking soda (bicarbonate of soda), an alkaline, is activated the moment it is mixed with an acid ingredient, such as sour cream or buttermilk. Because of this instantaneous reaction, a batter that contains baking soda should be baked right away, so the leavening occurs while baking in the oven.

Baking powder combines an alkaline and two acids (typically cream of tartar and sodium aluminum sulfate or a similar acid). Nearly all baking powder is labeled "double acting," which means that the two acids react at different times, one when combined with liquid and the other in the heat of the oven. While a baking-powder batter should be baked promptly, it doesn't demand the same urgency as baking soda because of the double action.

Cream of tartar, the common name for potassium tartrate, an acid, is used to stabilize egg whites so they will whip to great height. (If you're using a copper bowl, you can omit the cream of tartar because copper chemically interacts with the albumin in egg whites to stabilize them.) It also is added to some cake batters, such as Orange Chiffon Cake (page 74), to yield a delicate, whiter crumb and better loft.

Mechanical Leavening

Mechanical leavening is the introduction of air into a batter. It is the result of a physical motion, rather than the addition of a specific ingredient.

Creaming is the vigorous beating of a fat (such as butter) or a fat plus another ingredient (such as butter and sugar) to incorporate air, resulting in a light and fluffy mixture. In the case of the latter, the sharp, crystalline edges of the sugar cut into the butter, to create many tiny air bubbles that expand in the oven.

Foaming is the whipping of eggs with sugar to produce an airy, foamy mass. Once in the oven, the combination of trapped air, moisture, and heat produces steam, which causes the batter to rise.

Flavoring Ingredients

The most common flavorings are spices, extracts (essences), nuts, and fruits. Once you begin using them, you'll quickly discover that their flavors and aromas typically intensify during baking.

Basic ingredients, including butter and milk, that perform other critical roles also contribute to flavor. Eggs impart their signature flavor, too, mostly from the fat present in the yolk. The bacterial cultures in sour cream and buttermilk add tanginess, while cream cheese, made from whole milk and cream, is responsible for the distinctive taste of Vanilla Cheesecake (page 121).

Chocolate is probably the most popular flavoring, however. Most chocolate is nothing more than a mixture of varying amounts of chocolate liquor, sugar, and vanilla, plus milk solids for milk chocolate. Many of the world's most-treasured cakes owe their fame to its one-of-a-kind flavor.

Mixing, Flavoring & Baking Cakes

From the moment you take the flour off the shelf, making a cake requires close attention to detail. You need to start with the correct ingredients, at the correct temperature and in the correct amounts, and you must combine them in ways that enhance the overall flavor of the cake. Next, your oven must be in good working order, and finally, every carefully baked cake demands the same care in serving.

Mise en Place

The French phrase *mise en place* means "everything in its place," and it is a principal rule of cake making. Essentially, it calls for readying everything, ingredients and equipment, before you begin to make a recipe. First, read through the recipe carefully. Check the ingredients and put whatever you're missing on a shopping list. Check the equipment, too, and if you don't own the correct pan, for example, add it to the list. Then, at least 30 minutes before you begin to

make the cake, review the recipe again to see if butter, cream cheese, eggs, or any other refrigerated ingredients need to be brought to room temperature. Butter or cream cheese that has been allowed to warm up and thus soften slightly will combine more easily with other ingredients, resulting in smooth, fluffy batters and, in turn, better cakes. Eggs cold from the refrigerator are easier to separate, but egg whites that have been brought to room temperature will whip up more fully.

When it is time to begin baking, set out all the necessary equipment, from measuring cups to spoons to pans. Prepare the pans—with butter, butter and flour, parchment (baking) paper—if called for. Turn on the oven at least 20 minutes before the cake goes into it, so that it heats fully. Next, ready all the ingredients. This includes not only measuring them, but also perhaps sifting dry ingredients, grating citrus zest, squeezing juices, chopping chocolate, or the like. Review the recipe again to make sure you know the sequence of the steps and you have everything you need, then line up the ingredients in their order of use. Read up on any key techniques, such as separating an egg (page 36) or using a pastry (piping) bag (page 44), you haven't yet mastered or are new to you. You're now on your way to making a great cake.

Measuring Ingredients

A successful cake depends on measuring ingredients precisely. American home cooks are generally more comfortable using cups to measure both wet and dry ingredients, while professional bakers and many home bakers elsewhere in the world traditionally weigh their dry ingredients, especially when working with large amounts, knowing that weight is usually a more accurate measurement. Weights are also handy when you're shopping because they let you know how many ounces (grams) of walnut halves or shredded coconut to buy. All the recipes in this book have been tested with cup measurements, but weights are also included for all the dry ingredients, in case you want to use them.

When measuring dry ingredients, always use cups specially designed for

the task, which are usually metal or plastic and have thin, straight rims (page 133). There are two basic measuring methods, spoon and sweep and scoop and level. For the spoon and sweep method, which I prefer, use a spoon to fill the measuring cup to overflowing and then level the top with a thin metal spatula or the back of a table knife. For the scoop and level method, dip the cup into the ingredient and then level it. If a recipe gives a cup measure for sifted flour, be sure to sift the flour first and then measure it. Sifting aerates dry ingredients, which yields a different (lighter) amount. Sifting also breaks up tiny lumps and distributes small quantities of ingredients, like baking powder, evenly through a mixture. Select one measuring method and use it consistently. When using measuring spoons, dip them into the ingredient and then level them.

Liquid ingredients are measured in a clear glass or plastic cup with vertical markings indicating amounts. Pour the amount of liquid called for into the cup, put the cup on the countertop, let the contents settle, and then double-check the amount at eye level to be sure of an accurate reading. If using measuring

spoons, fill to the rim with the liquid.

To measure sticky ingredients such as honey or molasses, oil the measuring cup or spoon (or spray with nonstick cooking spray) before filling it. The thick liquid will slide out easily. Most butter wrappers are printed with markings indicating both tablespoons and partial cups, so you can cut off the amount you need.

Layering Flavors

Cakes with a particularly full, satisfying flavor owe their success primarily to two techniques: the layering of the same flavor and the use of one flavor or ingredient to bring out another flavor. Orange Chiffon Cake (page 74) is a good example of the layering of like flavors. The cake batter includes both orange juice and zest. That orange flavor is heightened by topping the cake with an orange glaze. Almond paste and almond extract (essence) work together to flavor the batter of Almond Pound Cake (page 55), while a scattering of sliced (flaked) almonds on top provides yet another layer of emphasis as well as texture. Triple Chocolate Layer Cake (page 110) layers devil's food cake, a ganache filling, and a creamy chocolate

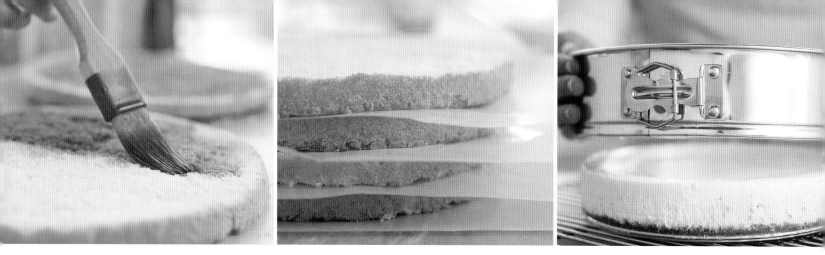

frosting to create a bold chocolate flavor in every bite. Chocolate-Berry Cake Roll (page 118) delivers the same triple flavor boost with its raspberry-flavored syrup and buttercream and fresh berries on top.

Using coffee to bring out the flavor of chocolate in Mocha Cake Roll (page 118), a combination of chocolate sponge cake and coffee buttercream, illustrates how one ingredient can intensify the flavor of another. A second example is the nutty-flavored brown butter in Brown-Butter Hazelnut Cakes (page 73), which mimics the toasted nuts in the batter. Even the spoonful of sugar tossed with the berries in Strawberry Roulade (page 119), is a good example of this flavoring technique as the sugar intensifies the strawberry flavor.

Monitoring Your Oven

There are two main types of ovens, the gas oven, which uses gas flames to generate radiant heat, and the electric oven, which uses electric elements to generate dry heat. Both types bake cakes equally well. A third type, which is more common in professional kitchens, the gas or electric convection oven, is outfitted with a fan that circulates the hot air during baking, producing even heat throughout the space. Cakes tend to cook more evenly and quickly and at lower temperatures in a convection oven.

If you're using a cake recipe written for a conventional oven, such as the recipes in this book, reduce the oven temperature by 25°F (15°C) and the time by 20 percent to adjust for a convection oven.

Use an oven thermometer, which can be kept in the oven at all times (page 134), to check your oven's accuracy. If it indicates that your oven is not heating to the correct temperature, compensate for the difference when you set the dial. If the problem cannot be corrected with this simple adjustment, have your oven checked professionally.

Unless specified, cakes are generally baked on the middle rack of the oven for the most even heat. Every oven has hot spots, however, and you need to learn where they are in your oven. For example, when you have two cake pans side by side, one may bake faster than the other because it is closer to the oven wall or a heat element, two typical hot spots. Check your cake pans halfway through baking and swap their positions if one cake layer seems to be baking faster than the other. If you're using a baking sheet, always rotate it 180 degrees at the midway point to compensate for uneven heating. Since individual ovens vary, baking times are only guidelines. Begin checking for doneness a couple of minutes before the shortest time the recipe indicates, to prevent overbaking.

High-Altitude Baking

Air pressure is lower at high altitudes where the air is thinner, so cakes bake differently that they do at lower altitudes. If you live in a high-altitude area, you need to adjust the amounts of leaveners and sugars slightly downward and the amounts of liquids slightly upward. You also need to increase oven temperatures and decrease baking times. Check with your local agricultural extension office for precise information.

Food Safety

A clean work surface and clean utensils will keep your cakes free of unwanted flavors and prevent bacterial contamination. Although the incidence of salmonella bacteria in eggs is statistically very low (1 out of 20,000), many cooks believe that precautions should be taken. To make sure any bacteria present are killed, mixtures containing eggs must be heated to 160°F (70°C), or they must be kept at 140°F (60°C) for 3 minutes. Recipes in this book that contain raw egg whites are indicated. In some cases, pasteurized egg whites can be substituted.

Serving Cakes

After all your hard work, your cake is now ready to be served. Most cakes taste best at room temperature—that's when frostings are soft and creamy, flavors are fullest, and textures are moist and tender. Cakes that are at the proper serving temperature will also be easier to slice. Equally important is cutting a nice, neat wedge for a beautiful presentation. Don't rush this step—you will be more pleased with the results if you take your time.

Serving Temperatures

At room temperature, cheesecakes are wonderfully rich and creamy, and the flavor of chocolate, whether filling, frosting, or cake, is at its most intense. Most layer cakes or rolled cakes that have been refrigerated should be removed about 30 minutes before serving. Most unfrosted cakes are typically stored at room temperature. Some cakes, such as a roulade filled and frosted with whipped cream, are served directly from the refrigerator because of their perishable ingredients.

Cutting Slices

To cut moist, firm-textured cakes, use a long, sharp thin-bladed knife and a smooth, flowing motion. Use the same knife to cut a dense cake, always dipping it in hot water before each cut and wiping it clean with a towel. To cut a light, airy cake, use a long, sharp serrated knife and a gentle sawing motion.

In general, a 9-inch (23-cm) layer cake or a 10-inch (25-cm) angel food cake can be cut into 10 to 12 servings. A pound cake baked in a large loaf pan yields about the same number of slices. Because of its richness, a 9-inch cheesecake will yield 16 servings.

To simplify cutting even slices from a round frosted cake, use a knife to make a shallow mark across the center of the top, dividing the cake in half. Now make a second shallow mark across the cake perpendicular to the first mark, yielding quarters. Finally, mark each quarter with additional marks, depending on how many slices you will need. Using your marks as guidelines, cut into servings.

1

Basic Recipes

Making a cake often calls for preparing a few different components and then putting them together. In this chapter, you will learn how to make the fillings and frostings you'll need, such as a smooth buttercream, a fluffy meringue, and a zesty lemon curd. You'll also master some of the final touches used to decorate cakes, including candied orange zest and sugared rose petals.

Vanilla Buttercream

When I want to dress up a special layer cake with a silky smooth finish, this frosting or filling is my hands-down choice. I start with a stable base of egg whites and sugar, and then I beat in softened butter and a spoonful of vanilla extract to create this classic smooth, creamy, full-flavored frosting.

3 cold large eggs, separated (page 36)

¼ teaspoon cream of tartar

⅔ cup (5 oz/155 g) plus 2 tablespoons granulated sugar

¼ cup (2 fl oz/60 fl oz) water

1 tablespoon light corn syrup

1¼ cups (10 oz/315 g) unsalted butter, at room temperature

1 tablespoon vanilla extract (essence)

MAKES ABOUT 4½ CUPS (36 FL OZ/1.1 L)

1 Prepare the egg whites

After separating the eggs, pour the egg whites into the bowl of a stand mixer or a mixing bowl and add the cream of tartar. Save the yolks for another use, such as Citrus Curd (page 26) or pastry cream (page 128). Using a whisk, stir together until the cream of tartar dissolves, then set aside while you cook the syrup.

2 Cook the sugar syrup

In a small, heavy-bottomed saucepan, combine the ⅔ cup sugar, the water, and the corn syrup. Clip a candy thermometer onto the pan and be sure the stem is submerged in liquid. Partially cover and place over low heat until the sugar dissolves, about 5 minutes. Uncover occasionally and stir with a wooden spoon to be sure it dissolves. Raise the heat to high and let the syrup bubble vigorously, without stirring, until it is smooth and thick and registers 240°F (116°C) on the thermometer, about 5 minutes. (This is called the *soft-ball stage*. To test without a thermometer, drop a small amount of syrup into ice water; if it forms a ball that holds its shape when pressed, it's ready). Using a damp pastry brush, wipe down any sugar crystals that form on the pan sides. Remove from the heat.

3 Whip the egg whites

If you need help whipping egg whites, turn to page 37. As soon as the syrup is off the heat, fit the mixer with the whip attachment and beat the egg white mixture with the 2 tablespoons sugar on medium speed until foamy, about 1 minute. Increase the speed to medium-high and continue beating until white, shiny, and smooth and the whip forms lines in the mixture, 2–3 minutes. Stop the mixer and lift the whip; the peaks of the whites should be slightly bent. These are *soft peaks*.

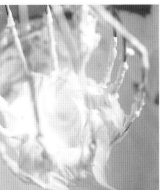
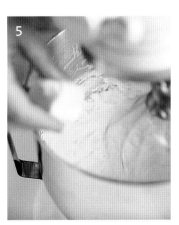

4 Add the hot sugar syrup to the egg whites

Reduce the mixer speed to low. Carefully pour the hot syrup in a thin stream in the space between the whip and the sides of the bowl. Pour slowly to prevent the sugar syrup from splashing onto the sides of the bowl and the whip. The outside of the bowl will feel hot to the touch. Increase the mixer speed to medium-low and beat continuously for 5 minutes. At this point, the outside of the bowl will be lukewarm and the peaks of the egg whites will be firm and straight, forming *stiff peaks*, when the whip is lifted. The mixture is now called a *meringue*.

5 Beat the butter into the meringue

Using the lines on the wrapper as a guide, cut the butter into 2-tablespoon pieces and remove the wrapper. Turn the mixer on medium-high speed and add the butter to the meringue 1 piece at a time, beating until each portion is incorporated before adding the next one. (If using a handheld mixer, move the beaters around in the bowl to make sure every bit of the mixture is well beaten.) If unbeaten butter sticks to the sides of the bowl, stop the mixer and use a rubber spatula to scrape it down into the rest of the mixture.

6 Adjust the consistency, if necessary

If the butter is too cold and forms tiny lumps, put the bowl over (not touching) hot water in a saucepan and stir vigorously until the lumps disappear and the buttercream is smooth again, then continue as directed. Add the vanilla extract and beat until evenly combined. The buttercream should be soft enough to spread, but not so soft that it pours. If it is too soft, refrigerate it for about 20 minutes until it firms up slightly, then, just before using, whisk for a few seconds until smooth.

7 Use or store the buttercream

Use the buttercream right away, or cover tightly and refrigerate for up to 3 days. If refrigerated, let stand at room temperature for about 1 hour to soften, then use a balloon whisk to whisk vigorously for about 1 minute. It should look smooth and fluffy.

PASTRY CHEF'S TIP

If when you pour the sugar syrup out of the pan, a thin sheet remains hardened on the bottom and sides, fill the pan three-fourths full of water, bring to a boil, and then pour out. This will remove the hardened syrup and make the pan easier to clean.

RECOMMENDED USES
Coconut Layer Cake (page 111), Banana Layer Cake (page 111), Mocha Cake Roll (page 118), Chocolate-Berry Cake Roll (page 118), and Pinwheel Cakes (page 119).

Chocolate Buttercream

BASIC RECIPE

Buttercream can be made in many different flavors. Here, melted chocolate is added to create a rich, smooth mixture. Like the vanilla version on page 20, this buttercream begins with a base of sugar and whipped egg whites enriched with softened butter. A touch of vanilla rounds out the chocolate flavor.

3 cold large eggs, separated (page 36)

8 oz (250 g) semisweet (plain) chocolate or white chocolate, chopped (page 40)

¼ teaspoon cream of tartar

⅔ cup (5 oz/155 g) plus 2 tablespoons granulated sugar

¼ cup (2 fl oz/60 fl oz) water

1 tablespoon light corn syrup

1¼ cups (10 oz/315 g) unsalted butter, at room temperature

1 teaspoon vanilla extract (essence)

MAKES ABOUT 4½ CUPS (36 FL OZ/1.1 L)

1 **Prepare the egg whites and melt the chocolate**
Pour the egg whites into the bowl of a stand mixer or a mixing bowl and add the cream of tartar. Save the yolks for another use. Using a whisk, stir until the cream of tartar dissolves. Set aside. Put the chocolate in a large, heatproof bowl and melt over (not touching) barely simmering water. (For more details, see page 40). Set aside.

2 **Cook the syrup**
In a small, heavy-bottomed saucepan, combine the ⅔ cup sugar, the water, and the corn syrup. Clip a candy thermometer onto the pan and be sure the stem is submerged in liquid. Partially cover and place over low heat until the sugar dissolves, about 5 minutes. Uncover occasionally and stir with a wooden spoon. Raise the heat to high and let the syrup bubble vigorously, without stirring, until it is smooth and thick and registers 240°F (116°C) on the thermometer, about 5 minutes. (This is called the *soft-ball stage*. To test without a thermometer, drop a small amount of syrup into ice water; if it forms a ball that holds its shape when pressed, it's ready). Using a damp pastry brush, wipe down any sugar crystals that form on the pan sides. Remove from the heat.

3 **Whip the egg whites**
If you need help whipping egg whites, turn to page 37. As soon as the syrup is off the heat, fit the mixer with the whip attachment and beat the egg white mixture with the 2 tablespoons sugar on medium speed until foamy, about 1 minute. Increase the speed to medium-high and continue beating until white, shiny, and smooth and the whip forms lines in the mixture, 2–3 minutes. Stop the mixer and lift the whip; the peaks of the whites should be slightly bent. These are *soft peaks*.

4 Add the hot sugar syrup to the egg whites

Reduce the mixer speed to low. Carefully pour the hot syrup in a thin stream in the space between the whip and the sides of the bowl. Pour slowly to prevent the sugar syrup from splashing onto the sides of the bowl and the whip. The outside of the bowl will feel hot to the touch. Increase the mixer speed to medium-low and beat continuously for 5 minutes. At this point, the outside of the bowl will be lukewarm and the peaks of the egg whites will be firm and straight, forming *stiff peaks*, when the whip is lifted. The mixture is now called a *meringue*.

5 Beat the butter and chocolate into the meringue

Using the lines on the wrappers as a guide, cut the butter into 2-tablespoon pieces and remove the wrapper. Turn the mixer on medium-high speed and add the butter to the meringue 1 piece at a time, beating until each portion is incorporated before adding the next one. Add the melted chocolate and beat well. (If using a handheld mixer, move the beaters around in the bowl to make sure every bit of the mixture is well beaten.) If unbeaten butter sticks to the sides of the bowl, use a rubber spatula to scrape it down into the rest of the mixture.

6 Adjust the consistency, if necessary

If the butter is too cold and forms tiny lumps, put the bowl over (not touching) hot water in a saucepan and stir vigorously until the lumps disappear and the buttercream is smooth again, then continue as directed. Add the vanilla extract and beat until evenly combined. The buttercream should be soft enough to spread, but not so soft that it pours. If it is too soft, refrigerate it for about 20 minutes until it firms up slightly, then, just before using, whisk for a few seconds until smooth.

7 Use or store the buttercream

Use the buttercream right away, or tightly cover and refrigerate for up to 3 days. If refrigerated, let stand at room temperature for about 1 hour to soften, then use a balloon whisk to whisk vigorously for about 1 minute. It should look smooth and fluffy.

MAKE-AHEAD TIP

Leftover buttercream can be frozen in an airtight container for up to 1 month. Before using, uncover and let it sit at room temperature until softened. Once the buttercream is soft, use a balloon whisk to whisk until it is once again soft and fluffy.

RECOMMENDED USES
Classic Birthday Cake (page 105), Double Chocolate Layer Cake (page 110), and Bûche de Noël (page 113).

Meringue Frosting

Fluffy and marshmallow-like, this old-fashioned frosting is made by beating egg whites and sugar in a bowl over hot water until the mixture thickens and increases in volume. The result is a soft, glossy, snow-white frosting that is not too rich and almost spreads itself.

3 cold large eggs

1¼ cups (10 oz/315 g) granulated sugar

⅓ cup (3 fl oz/80 ml) water

¼ teaspoon cream of tartar

1 teaspoon vanilla extract (essence)

¼ teaspoon almond extract (essence)

MAKES ABOUT 5½ CUPS (44 FL OZ/1.35 L)

1 Set up a double boiler
Pour water to a depth of 1 inch (2.5 cm) into a saucepan. Create a double boiler by placing a metal bowl in the top of the saucepan. Make sure that the bowl fits snugly in the rim and that its bottom does not touch the water. Remove the bowl from the pan and set it on the work surface.

2 Separate the eggs
For more details on separating eggs, turn to page 36. Have ready 2 small bowls. Holding an egg in one hand, strike it sharply on its equator on the work surface, cracking it, then hold it upright over 1 small bowl and lift away the top half of the shell. The yolk should be resting in the bottom half. Working gently so as not to break the yolk and holding the shell halves, cupped side up, over the bowl, move the yolk back and forth between the halves, allowing all the egg white to drop into the bowl. Then drop the yolk into the second small bowl, and transfer the white to the metal bowl. Repeat with the remaining 2 eggs. Reserve the yolks for another use, such as Citrus Curd (page 26) or pastry cream (page 128).

3 Beat the egg white mixture until foamy
Add the sugar, water, and cream of tartar to the bowl with the egg whites. Using a handheld mixer fitted with the whip attachment, beat the mixture on high speed until opaque white and foamy, about 1 minute.

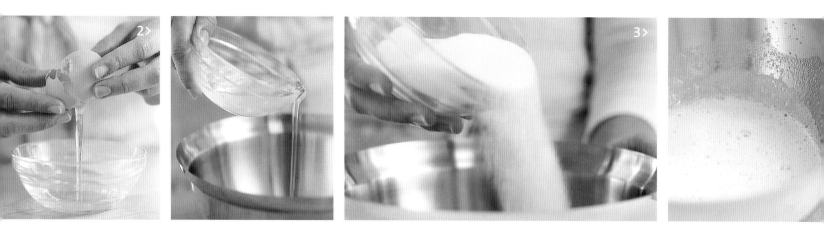

4 Beat the frosting over hot water

Place the saucepan over low heat, and heat just until you see small bubbles break the surface of the water. Place the bowl holding the egg white mixture in the pan. Check again to make sure the bowl does not touch the water, or you will overcook the frosting. Using the mixer, and moving the whip around in the bowl to reach every bit of egg white, beat on high speed until white, shiny, and smooth and the movement of the whip forms lines in the mixture, about 7 minutes. While mixing, be sure to keep the mixer cord away from the burner. At this point, if you stop the mixer and lift the whip, the peaks of the whites should be slightly bent; these are *soft peaks*. The mixture is now called a *meringue*.

5 Finish the frosting

Using pot holders, carefully transfer the bowl to a work surface. Pour in the vanilla and almond extracts and continue to beat the frosting on medium speed, moving the whip around to reach all areas of the bowl to thicken the frosting further, about 2 minutes. When the frosting is ready, it will form billowy peaks when the whip is lifted from the bowl. Use the frosting right away.

PASTRY CHEF'S TIP

If you are unsure about the freshness of your eggs, put them in a bowl of cold water. If the eggs sink to the bottom and lie on their sides, they are fresh. If they float or stand on one end, the eggs are past their prime.

RECOMMENDED USES
Lemon Meringue Cake (page 110). You can also use this frosting on Devil's Food Cake (page 100) for an attractive contrasting color and flavor.

Citus Curd

BASIC RECIPE

Citrus Curd

These thick, smooth, citrus-flavored mixtures can be used as fillings for layer cakes or cake rolls, or combined with whipped cream for fluffy frostings. The addition of egg yolks along with whole eggs gives the curd a particularly rich flavor. Choose lemons, limes, or oranges, depending on the desired flavor.

3 or 4 lemons, 4 or 5 limes, or 2 or 3 oranges, preferably organic

2 large eggs plus 2 large egg yolks

1 cup (8 oz/250 g) granulated sugar

6 tablespoons (3 oz/90 g) unsalted butter, at room temperature

MAKES ABOUT 1½ CUPS (12 FL OZ/375 ML)

1 **Remove the citrus zest**
If you need help zesting or juicing citrus, turn to page 35. With a stiff-bristled brush, scrub the citrus under running cold water, especially if you have not purchased organic fruits. Place a fine rasp grater over a small bowl. Carefully draw 1 fruit across the grater, removing just the colored portion of the peel, called the *zest*. Take care not to remove the white *pith* below, as it is bitter. Continue to draw the fruit across the rasps, rotating as necessary, until all the zest has been removed. Repeat with additional fruits to yield a total of 2 teaspoons zest. Set aside.

2 **Squeeze the juice from the citrus**
Working with 1 fruit, cut in half crosswise. Using a reamer held over a bowl or a citrus juicer, juice each half. Pour the expressed juice through a fine-mesh sieve held over a glass measuring cup, to remove any impurities and seeds. Repeat with additional fruits to yield a total of ½ cup (4 fl oz/125 ml) juice.

3 **Set up a double boiler**
Pour water to a depth of 1 inch (2.5 cm) into a saucepan. Create a double boiler by placing a metal bowl in the top of the saucepan. Make sure that the bowl fits snugly in the rim and that its bottom does not touch the water. Remove the bowl from the pan and set it on the work surface.

4 **Mix the curd ingredients**
Add the citrus juice, whole eggs, egg yolks, and sugar to the bowl. Using a whisk, stir together until smoothly blended. Cut the butter into 12 equal pieces and add them to the mixture, but resist the urge to stir.

26 BASIC RECIPES

5   Cook the curd

Place the saucepan over low heat, and heat until you see small bubbles break the surface of the water. Place the bowl holding the egg mixture in the pan. Check again to make sure the bowl does not touch the water. Cook the mixture over the simmering water, stirring constantly and gently with a large wooden spoon or heatproof spatula, until the butter melts and the curd has thickened, about 8 minutes. To ensure a smooth and evenly cooked sauce, be sure to stir often, especially around the bottom and sides of the pan. (If you did not bring the butter to room temperature, the curd will take a few more minutes to thicken.) From time to time, use pot holders to lift the bowl and make sure the water is still at a simmer. Do not allow the water to boil, or the curd will cook too quickly, causing lumps to form. Also take care not to stir too vigorously, or the curd will be runny rather than nicely thickened.

6   Check the consistency of the curd

To test if the curd has thickened sufficiently, pull the spoon from the curd and draw your finger down the center of the back; a trail should remain that does not fill immediately. (You can also test with an instant-read thermometer, it should register 165°F (74°C) when it's inserted into the mixture.)

7   Strain and chill the curd

Suspend a fine-mesh sieve over a bowl, and carefully pour the curd through the sieve. Any stray lumps will be trapped in the sieve. Discard the solids in the sieve. Stir the citrus zest into the strained curd. Press a piece of plastic wrap directly onto the surface of the strained curd. This prevents a film from forming on top of the curd as it sets up in the refrigerator. Using a toothpick, poke a few holes in the plastic to let steam escape. Refrigerate until well chilled, which will take about 3 hours. It will thicken further as it cools.

8   Use or store the curd

Use the chilled curd right away, or store it in an airtight container in the refrigerator for up to 3 days.

MAKE-AHEAD TIP

To freeze citrus curd, put the chilled curd into an airtight container. Press plastic wrap directly onto the surface of the curd and cover tightly. Freeze for up to 1 month. Because the curd has a dense texture with a low moisture content, there is no need to thaw it. When ready to use, spoon out exactly what you need whenever you need it.

RECOMMENDED USES

Lemon Meringue Cake (page 110), Coconut Layer Cake (page 111), and Orange Cream Cake Roll (page 119).

Ganache

BASIC RECIPE

When freshly made, this smooth mixture of chocolate, cream, and butter
is a thick, pourable warm chocolate sauce that makes a delicious accompaniment
for cake slices. Once cooled, it can be a thick fudge filling. When chilled, it thickens
a bit more, becoming an ultracreamy frosting.

8 oz (250 g) semisweet (plain) or bittersweet
chocolate

2 tablespoons unsalted butter

⅔ cup (5 fl oz/160 ml) heavy (double) cream,
plus more as needed to adjust the consistency

1 teaspoon vanilla extract (essence)

MAKES ABOUT 1½ CUPS (12 FL OZ/375 ML)

1 Chop the chocolate

If you are new to chopping chocolate, turn to page 40. Place the chocolate
on a cutting board. Grasp the handle of a serrated knife or chef's knife with one
hand and, with your other hand placed about midpoint on the back of the blade,
cut the chocolate into large chunks. (You don't want to touch the chocolate with
your hand, as it could cause the chocolate to melt.) Then, move your hand closer
to the front end of the back of the blade, and using a rocking motion, cut the
chocolate into even pieces. Be sure the pieces are small so that they will melt
quickly. Set the chocolate aside.

2 Heat the butter and cream

Cut the butter into 2 equal pieces. In a heavy saucepan over medium-low
heat, combine the ⅔ cup cream and the butter. Heat until the butter is melted
and tiny bubbles have formed along the edges of the pan, about 2 minutes. The
mixture should register about 160°F (71°C) on an instant-read thermometer.
Do not allow the mixture to boil, or it could scorch and give the finished ganache
a burned taste.

3 Mix the chocolate with the remaining ingredients

Remove the pan from the heat and immediately add the chopped chocolate.
Let the chocolate sit in the hot cream mixture for about 30 seconds to soften.

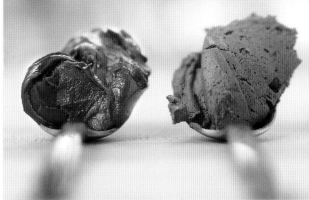

4 Mix the ganache
Add the vanilla extract to the chocolate-cream mixture. Using a whisk, blend the mixture in a circular motion until all the chocolate is melted and the mixture is smooth.

5 Let the ganache cool to the desired texture
At this point, the mixture will be smooth and pourable. Use it right away as a fudge sauce to accompany cake slices, or let it cool slightly, 10–15 minutes, for a pourable glaze for a whole cake. For a thicker fudge filling, let the mixture cool to room temperature, 1–2 hours, depending on how warm your kitchen is. It will thicken evenly and remain spreadable, clinging nicely to an icing spatula for easy application. If you want to use the ganache as a frosting, let cool completely: Using a heatproof silicone spatula, scrape the room temperature mixture into a large bowl and press a piece of plastic wrap directly onto the surface. Refrigerate until cool to the touch, thick, and firm around the edges, about 1 hour, stirring once after about 30 minutes to ensure that the mixture chills evenly.

6 Whip the mixture, if desired
Remove the chilled ganache from the refrigerator and, using a whisk, whip the chilled mixture until it changes from a dark to a medium chocolate color and becomes very creamy, about 30 seconds. When compared to the unwhipped mixture, the whipped mixture will be light brown and fluffy. The whipped mixture firms up quickly, so use it as soon as possible.

PASTRY CHEF'S TIP
If your finished ganache looks curdled, or broken, heat it again over a double boiler and let melt. Chill for 30 minutes in the refrigerator and whisk to bring it back to the desired consistency.

RECOMMENDED USES
As a sauce for slices of Angel Food Cake (page 57), as filling for Triple Chocolate Layer Cake (page 110), and as a flavoring for Chocolate Cheesecake (page 126), or Marble Cheesecake (page 127).

Candied Citrus Zest
& Sugared Flowers

Sweet, tangy strips of candied zest and colorful candied flowers placed on or around a cake add a unique finishing touch. Both are easy to prepare and can be made in advance, and they can be used to decorate nearly any cake. Follow steps 1–3 to make the candied zest, or steps 4–6 for the sugared flowers.

For the candied citrus zest

2 oranges, lemons, or limes

⅔ cup (5 fl oz/160 ml) water

2 tablespoons cider vinegar

½ cup (4 oz/125 g) granulated sugar

MAKES ABOUT 2–3 TABLESPOONS ZEST

For the candied flowers

3 tablespoons pasteurized egg whites

3 tablespoons superfine (caster) sugar

20–25 small pesticide-free edible flowers or flower petals such as pansies or rose petals

MAKES 20–25 FLOWERS

1 **Remove the zest from the fruit**
Using a vegetable peeler and a light sawing motion, remove the colored part of the peel, called the *zest*, from each fruit in long, wide strips. Leave as much of the bitter white *pith* on the fruit as you can. Using a small, sharp knife, trim off any of the pith that remains on the zest, then use a chef's knife to cut the zest into matchstick-sized strips. Discard any small or odd-shaped pieces.

2 **Simmer the zest strips**
In a small saucepan, combine the zest strips with enough water to just cover them and place over high heat. As soon as you see large bubbles start to form, remove the pan from the heat, pour into a sieve held over the sink, and then hold the sieve under running cold water to cool the strips and help set the color. In the same pan over medium heat, combine the ⅔ cup (5 fl oz/160 ml) water, vinegar, and granulated sugar. Heat until small bubbles begin to form on the surface of the liquid and stir to dissolve the sugar. Add the citrus strips and continue to simmer until the zest softens and the liquid thickens slightly, about 10 minutes.

3 **Use or store the candied zest**
If using the candied zest immediately, pour into a sieve to drain, discarding the syrup. If not using immediately, transfer the slightly cooled zest and syrup to a small bowl, cover, and refrigerate for up to 1 week, then drain and discard the syrup before using the zest.

4 Paint the flowers with egg white

Cover a wire rack with parchment (baking) paper. In a small bowl, whisk the eggs whites until foamy, about 1 minute. (I like to use pasteurized whites instead of fresh ones to reduce the risk of salmonella.) Put the superfine sugar in another small bowl. Using a clean paintbrush, dip it in the egg whites and lightly and evenly coat one flower or petal with the whites. I paint the top side only, but if you prefer a stiffer flower or petal, paint both sides.

5 Sprinkle the petals with sugar

Sprinkle the egg white–coated flower or petal lightly and evenly with a little of the sugar, then gently shake any excess sugar back into the bowl. Place the flower or petal, sugar side up (if only one side is sugared), on the prepared rack. Repeat the process with the remaining flowers or petals, then let stand in a cool, dry place to dry completely, at least 4 hours or up to overnight. (If the weather is hot and humid, dry them in an air-conditioned room.)

6 Use or store the candied flowers

Use the flowers right away or store them. To store, arrange between layers of parchment or waxed paper in an airtight tin, stacking them no more than 4 layers high, and keep in a dry place for up to 2 weeks or in the freezer for up to 3 months.

PASTRY CHEF'S TIP

Other flowers with small blossoms and simple configurations, such as violets and Peruvian lilies, are good choices for sugaring. Be sure to buy flowers that are grown for consumption. If you have any doubt that they are pesticide free, do not use them.

RECOMMENDED USES

To garnish Pound Cake (page 49), Angel Food Cake (page 57), and Classic Birthday Cake (page 105).

2

Key Techniques

This chapter, rich in instructional text and photographs, explains various techniques that are indispensable to making cakes, fillings, and frostings, such as how to chop and melt chocolate, whip egg whites, and grate citrus zest. You'll also learn the best ways to butter and flour cake and sheet pans, unmold a baked cake, and, finally, fill, frost, and decorate your beautiful homemade cake.

Preparing Cake Pans

1 Butter the pan
Place a small amount of soft unsalted butter on a piece of waxed paper and spread over the bottom and sides of a round cake pan, generously coating the entire surface.

2 Fold parchment (baking) paper
For a 9-inch (23-cm) pan, cut an 11-inch (28-cm) square of parchment paper and fold it into quarters to make a smaller square. Fold the square in half to make a triangle.

3 Press parchment paper into pan
Position the point of the triangle in the center of the pan, unfold it slightly, and press it into the pan so that a crease forms along the edge.

4 Cut the parchment paper
Remove the creased parchment paper from the pan. Use scissors to cut along the crease. Unfold the paper, which should form a circle that fits in the bottom of the pan.

5 Butter the parchment paper
Place the cut parchment paper back in the bottom of the buttered pan. Again, place a small amount of soft butter on a piece of waxed paper and spread the butter over the paper.

6 Flour the pan, if called for
Add 2 tablespoons flour to the pan, then tilt and shake it so the flour coats the butter evenly. Invert the pan over the sink and tap it to release excess flour.

Preparing Sheet Pans

1 Butter the pan

Place a small amount of soft unsalted butter on a piece of waxed paper and spread over the bottom and sides of the pan. Cut parchment (baking) paper to fit and place in the pan.

Zesting & Juicing Citrus

1 Zest the lemon

If you are zesting and juicing a lemon, zest it first. Use a rasp grater or the grating teeth on a box grater-shredder to remove only the colored part of the peel, not the bitter white pith.

2 Clean off the grater

Don't forget to scrape all the zest from the back of a grater, where some of it naturally gathers.

2 Finish preparing the pan

Butter the parchment paper. Add 2 tablespoons flour, and tilt and shake the pan to coat evenly. Invert the pan over the sink and tap it to release excess flour.

3 Slice the lemon in half

To juice a lemon, first press and roll it firmly against a countertop to break some of the membranes holding in the juice. Then, using a chef's knife, cut the fruit in half crosswise.

4 Juice the lemon

To extract as much juice as possible, use a citrus reamer to pierce the membranes as you squeeze. Catch the juice in a bowl, and strain to remove seeds before using.

Separating Eggs

1 Crack the egg
Eggs are easiest to separate when cold. Have 3 clean, grease-free bowls ready. To reduce shell fragments, crack the side of the egg sharply on a flat surface, rather than the rim of a bowl.

2 Pull apart the shell halves
Hold the cracked egg over an empty bowl and carefully pull the shell apart, letting the white (but not the yolk) start to drop into the bowl.

3 Pass the yolk back and forth
Transfer the yolk back and forth from one shell half to the other, letting the white fall away completely into the bowl below. Be careful not to break the yolk on a sharp shell edge.

4 Put the yolk in another bowl
Gently drop the yolk into the second bowl. Keeping the whites free of any yolk is key if you plan to whip the whites. A trace of yolk or other fat will prevent them from foaming.

TROUBLESHOOTING
If a yolk breaks as you separate the egg and gets into the white, this egg white cannot be used for whipping. Reserve the white for another use (like making scrambled eggs) or discard it. Rinse the bowl before continuing.

5 Put the white in another bowl
If the egg separates cleanly, pour the white into the third bowl. Break each new egg over the first empty bowl to avoid spoiling a batch of whites.

Whipping Egg Whites

TECHNIQUE

1 Beat the egg whites
Fit a mixer with the whip attachment. Beat room-temperature egg whites with cream of tartar on medium speed until foamy and the cream of tartar dissolves, about 1 minute.

2 Check for the soft-peak stage
Increase the speed to medium-high and beat until the whites look opaque but moist, 2–3 minutes. Stop beating and lift the whip: The whites should form slightly bent peaks.

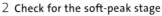

3 Check for the stiff peak stage
Continue to beat until the whites look glossy, 1–2 minutes longer. When the whip is lifted, they should hold a firm, straight peak. Take care not to overbeat.

TROUBLESHOOTING
Overbeaten egg whites appear grainy and can separate. Be sure to watch closely while beating. If you beat the egg whites to this stage, discard them and start again with fresh egg whites.

Ribbon Stage

TECHNIQUE

1 Beat the egg-sugar mixture
Fit a mixer with the twin beaters or the paddle. Beat the eggs and sugar on medium-high speed until mixed and increased in volume. Pay close attention to the changing mixture as you beat.

2 Check for the ribbon stage
The mixture will change from bright to pale yellow. The beaters or paddle will form lines in the thick, fluffy mixture, and the batter, when lifted, will fall back on itself like a ribbon.

Whipping Cream

1 Pour the cream into a bowl
Pour cold heavy (double) cream into a glass or stainless-steel bowl. For best results, chill the bowl as well, especially on a warm day. Add any sugar or flavoring called for in the recipe.

2 Whip the cream to soft peaks
Fit a mixer with the whip attachment. Beat the cream mixture on medium-high speed until it forms soft (slightly bent) peaks when you stop the mixer and lift the whip, about 3–4 minutes.

Creaming Butter

1 Combine the butter and sugar
Fit a mixer with twin beaters or the paddle attachment. Add room-temperature butter, cut into pieces, and sugar to a large bowl. Engage the mixer on medium speed.

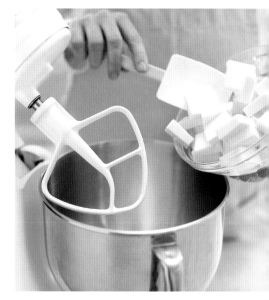

TROUBLESHOOTING
It's a good idea to stop the mixer often and check the consistency of the whipped cream. When cream is whipped too long, it becomes stiff and grainy and has a curdled appearance.

3 Fix overwhipped cream
If you mistakenly overwhip the cream, add a small amount of unwhipped cream and beat gently to bring back the soft peaks. Gradually add more cream if needed.

2 Creaming the mixture
Beat until light and fluffy, about 2 minutes. The mixture will change from light yellow to cream and have the consistency of stiffly whipped cream.

Folding Together Two Mixtures

TECHNIQUE

1 Add some of the light mixture
Folding is a crucial technique that combines two ingredients or mixtures with different densities. Pile one-third of the lighter mixture on top of the mixture that is to be folded.

2 Slice down the center through both mixtures
Using a rubber spatula and holding it vertically, slice down through the center of the mixtures to the bottom of the bowl.

3 Bring the spatula up one side
Turn the spatula horizontally, so it lies on the bottom of the bowl. Pull it along the bottom and up the side, keeping it flat against the side.

4 Fold the batter
Pull the spatula up and over the lighter mixture on top, bringing some of the heavier mixture from the bottom with it. Rotate the bowl a quarter turn and repeat the folding action.

5 Finish the folding process
Repeat this folding action, rotating the bowl each time, until no white streaks remain. Once the batter is lightened, fold in the rest of the light mixture by repeating steps 1–5.

TROUBLESHOOTING
It's natural for the batter to deflate slightly during folding. Be sure to work quickly and stop folding when the mixtures are just combined. Overly deflated batter will affect the cake's texture.

Chopping Chocolate

1 Cut the chocolate into chunks
Grasp the handle of a serrated or chef's knife with one hand and, with your other hand placed midpoint on the back of the blade, cut the chocolate into medium-sized pieces.

Melting Chocolate

1 Put the chocolate in a bowl
Using a bench scraper, transfer the chopped chocolate to a metal bowl that fits on the rim of a saucepan. Add other ingredients, such as butter, if called for in the recipe.

2 Set up a double boiler
Pour water to a depth of about 1½ inches (4 cm) into the saucepan. Heat on low until it barely simmers. Place the bowl on top, making sure the bottom doesn't touch the water.

2 Chop the chocolate into pieces
Moving your other hand closer to the front of the blade, rock the knife to cut the chocolate into small, even pieces. The smaller and more uniform the pieces, the easier they will melt.

3 Melt the chocolate
Heat the chocolate, stirring often with a heatproof spatula, until melted and smooth, about 3–4 minutes. Using pot holders, lift out the bowl. Let the chocolate cool for 5 minutes.

TROUBLESHOOTING
Chocolate can *seize* when it comes into contact with moisture, such as drops of water, during melting. To salvage it, remove it from the heat and stir in 1 tablespoon water at a time until the chocolate is smooth again.

Releasing Round Cakes from Pans

1 Cool the cake in the pan
Put the just-baked cake on a wire rack and let cool in the pan for 15 minutes. Wire racks allow air to circulate on all sides of the cake pan, which speeds cooling and prevents sogginess.

2 Loosen the cake from the pan
Run a thin knife along the inside edge of the pan to loosen the cake, keeping the knife pressed against the pan sides so it won't cut into the cake.

Releasing Sheet Cakes from Pans

1 Cool and loosen the cake
Follow steps 1 and 2 for releasing round cakes, letting the sheet cake cool in the pan for 25 minutes.

3 Invert the pan
Place another wire rack upside down on the cake pan. Using pot holders, grasp the rack and pan together and invert them in one quick movement.

4 Lift the pan off the cake
When cool enough to touch, lift the pan away from the cake. The cake will release from the pan. Then, peel off the paper and discard. Let the cake cool until cool to the touch.

2 Invert and lift off the pan
Follow step 3 for releasing a round cake. Lift the sheet pan off the cake and peel off and discard the paper. Let the cake cool until cool to the touch.

Cutting Two Round Cakes into Layers

TECHNIQUE

1 Measure the height
Place the cake on a cool work surface. Hold a ruler alongside it to measure its height and note the midpoint. If the cake isn't even on all sides, try to find an average.

2 Mark the layers with toothpicks
Using toothpicks, mark the midpoint of the cake at 4–6 equally spaced intervals around the cake. The picks will guide you as you cut the cake into 2 equal layers.

3 Split the cake into layers
Using a long serrated knife and a sawing motion, cut the layer horizontally to make 2 layers. Don't worry if the layers are uneven; they can be masked with filling or frosting.

4 Place the layers on waxed paper
Place a large sheet of waxed paper on a countertop, lift off the top cake layer and place it on the waxed paper while you cut the second cake.

5 Split the second layer
Follow steps 1–4 to split the second cake into 2 even layers.

6 Prepare to assemble the cake
Look at the cake layers and determine the order in which they will be layered. Put any uneven layers in the center of the cake, and reserve one of the smooth cake tops for the top tier.

Filling & Frosting a Four-Layer Cake

1 Brush the layers with syrup
Using a pastry brush, brush each layer with about 3 tablespoons syrup. Transfer a layer to a cake stand or plate. Slip 4 waxed paper strips under the edges of the cake.

2 Fill the layers
Mound one-third of the filling on the cake layer and spread evenly to the edges. Top evenly with another layer. Repeat with the remaining filling and layers, ending with the fourth layer.

3 Spread on the crumb coat
Using a clean offset icing spatula and about 1 cup (8 fl oz/250 ml) frosting, spread a thin layer of frosting over the top and sides of the cake to seal in the crumbs and create a smooth surface.

4 Mound more frosting on the cake
Clean the spatula to remove any stray crumbs, then use it to mound half of the remaining frosting on the center of the top of the cake.

5 Spread the frosting over the top
Using broad strokes, spread the frosting evenly over the top of the cake. Wipe the spatula frequently against the edge of the bowl holding the frosting to remove any excess.

6 Spread the frosting over the sides
Apply the remaining frosting in small batches to the sides of the cake, turning the plate as needed to frost the sides evenly. Smooth the top one last time to remove any unevenness.

Filling a Pastry Bag

TECHNIQUE

1 Fit the tip into the bag
Fit a decorating tip in the hole in the pastry bag. Depending on the bag's manufacturer, you may need to use a small, white device called a *coupler* to hold it in place.

2 Fold down the pastry bag
Using both hands, fold down the top of the bag to form a cuff. The cuff should be about one-third the length of the bag. This will make it easier to fill with frosting.

3 Fill the bag with frosting
Place one hand under the cuff of the pastry bag. Using a rubber spatula, scoop the frosting into the bag, filling it no more than half full.

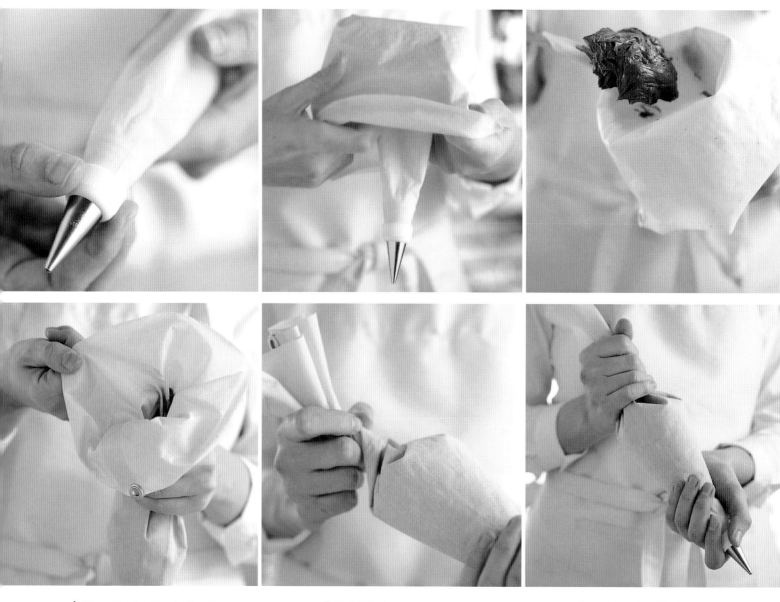

4 Move the frosting to the tip
Unfold the cuff. Push the frosting down toward the tip, forcing out any air at the same time. Trapped air bubbles can cause problems when piping.

5 Twist the bag
To further ensure against air bubbles, and to keep the frosting flowing well, twist the bag several times at the point where the frosting ends.

6 Position the filled pastry bag
Hold the top of the bag where the frosting stops with your dominant hand. With your non-dominant hand, hold the bag near the tip.

Piping with a Pastry Bag

1 Hold the bag at an angle
Use your upper hand to apply pressure, and the lower to guide the tip. Hold the bag with the tip 1 inch (2.5 cm) above and at a 60-degree angle to the cake.

2 To pipe rosettes:
Using the *star tip*, apply gentle pressure to pipe a mound ½ inch (12 mm) wide. Pull the bag up, lessening the pressure and lowering the angle. Repeat to form a row of rosettes.

Chocolate Curls

1 Run a peeler over the chocolate
Soften the chocolate by holding it in your hands for a minute or two. Holding the chocolate with one hand, use a vegetable peeler to scrape curls 1½–2 inches (4–5 cm) long.

3 To pipe shells:
Using the *fluted tip*, pipe a mound about ½ inch long. Pull the bag up, lessening the pressure and lowering the angle slightly. Repeat to form a row of shells.

4 To pipe dots:
Using a *small plain tip*, pipe a small mound of frosting, lifting up the bag to make a point on the top. Repeat to form the desired pattern of dots.

2 Let the shavings fall onto a pan
Turn the chocolate block so that you scrape from all sides, letting the chocolate curls fall in a single layer onto a rimmed baking sheet lined with parchment (baking) paper.

3

Simple Cakes

In this chapter, the focus of each recipe is on the cake itself, each of which requires little, if any, frosting, filling, or decoration. Classics such as pound cake and angel food cake fall into this category, as do such popular fruit- and vegetable-based cakes as apple cake, pineapple upside-down cake, and carrot cake. You'll also find miniature hazelnut (filbert) cakes and a rich flourless chocolate cake.

Pound Cake

In the past, pound cake recipes called for a pound (500 g) each of butter, sugar, eggs, and flour. While the proportions have changed, the basic method has remained the same: the steady, thorough beating of the butter and sugar and then the eggs guarantees the cake's signature dense, yet light structure.

1 Preheat the oven and prepare the pans

Position a rack in the middle of the oven, so the cakes will be evenly surrounded with heat, and preheat to 325°F (165°C). Place a small amount of butter on a piece of waxed paper and spread the butter evenly over the bottom and sides of two 8½-by-4½-inch (21.5-by-11.5-cm) loaf pans. Cut a piece of parchment (baking) paper to fit the pan and place it in the pan bottom. Butter the paper, then sprinkle lightly with flour. Tap out the excess flour. For more details on preparing pans, turn to page 34.

2 Sift the dry ingredients

Suspend a fine-mesh sieve over a bowl and add the flour, baking powder, and salt. Lightly tap the rim of the sieve to encourage the ingredients to pass into the bowl. This both combines the ingredients and aerates the flour (compacted flour produces a less tender texture, or *crumb*). Set the bowl aside.

3 Cream the butter and sugar

In the bowl of a stand mixer or a large mixing bowl, combine the butter and granulated sugar. Fit a stand mixer with the paddle attachment or a handheld mixer with the twin beaters. Beat the butter and sugar on medium speed until light and airy and the mixture changes in color from light yellow to cream, about 3 minutes. If using a handheld mixer, move the beaters around in the bowl to evenly beat the mixture. Stop the mixer occasionally and use a rubber spatula to scrape any unbeaten butter from the sides of the bowl. For more details on creaming butter, turn to page 38. >

Unsalted butter and flour for preparing the pans

4 cups (1¼ lb/625 g) all-purpose (plain) flour

1 teaspoon baking powder

½ teaspoon salt

2 cups (1 lb/500 g) unsalted butter, at room temperature

2¾ cups (22 oz/690 g) granulated sugar

8 large eggs

1 tablespoon vanilla extract (essence)

About 2 tablespoons confectioners' (icing) sugar, optional

MAKES TWO 8½-BY-4½-INCH (21.5-BY-11.5-CM) LOAF CAKES, OR 12 SERVINGS

PASTRY CHEF'S TIP

To make sure your butter is at room temperature, lightly press on it with a clean fingertip. If it leaves an imprint, the butter is ready to use.

4 »

4 Beat in the eggs and vanilla extract

Break the eggs into a small bowl and, using a fork, beat the eggs until the yolks and whites are blended. Add about ¼ cup (2 fl oz/60 ml) of the beaten eggs to the butter mixture and beat on medium speed until incorporated. Repeat with the remaining beaten eggs in 3 equal portions, beating well after each addition until incorporated before adding the next portion. Add the vanilla extract and mix well. As you near the end of mixing, the batter may look slightly curdled because the cold eggs may firm up the bits of butter. Do not worry. Continue beating for 2 minutes until the mixture warms and looks light and fluffy.

5 Mix in the dry ingredients

Reduce the mixer speed to low and slowly add half of the dry ingredients, beating just until the flour mixture is incorporated and no white streaks are visible. Beat in the remaining dry ingredients in the same manner. The batter will be smooth and thick and any slight curdling will have disappeared.

6 Bake the cakes

Pour the batter into the prepared pans, dividing it evenly. Use a rubber spatula to scrape every last bit from the bowl, then smooth the surfaces lightly. They do not need to be perfectly smooth; the tops become smooth during baking. Bake undisturbed for 1 hour. If the cakes look set—that is, the batter no longer looks liquid and the top is lightly browned—touch the tops gently. If they feel firm, insert a thin skewer or toothpick in the centers. If it comes out dry, the cakes are done. If it comes out wet or with crumbs clinging to it, set the timer for another 5 minutes, continue to bake, and check again. Repeat this process until the cakes test done. They will probably take a total of 1 hour and 10 minutes, but the timing may vary 2 or 3 minutes depending on the cakes' positions in the oven.

PASTRY CHEF'S TIP

If tiny egg shell fragments fall into the bowl of egg whites or yolks, scoop them up with an emptied half shell. They readily cling to it, and it works better than your fingers or a spoon or knife tip.

7 Let the cakes cool

Using pot holders, carefully transfer the cakes to a wire rack. Let cool in the pans for 30 minutes. Then, unmold the cakes: run a thin knife along the inside edge of the pans to loosen each cake, keeping the knife pressed against the pan sides. Invert a wire rack on top of 1 cake and invert them together. The cake will release from the pan. Repeat with the second cake. Lift off the pans, then peel off the parchment and discard it. (For more details on releasing cakes from pans, turn to page 41.) Using both hands, carefully turn the cakes top side up on the rack and let cool completely, about 1½ hours.

MAKE-AHEAD TIP

This cake can be frozen for up to 3 months. Let it cool completely, omit dusting it with confectioners' (icing) sugar, wrap tightly in plastic wrap, and then in heavy-duty aluminum foil. Thaw at room temperature before serving.

8 Serve or store the cakes

If desired, pour the confectioners' sugar into a fine-mesh sieve and lightly tap the rim of the sieve to release a fine dusting of sugar over the cakes. Use only enough sugar to coat the tops lightly. The fine coating of sugar lends a simple, finished look to the cakes. Carefully slide the cakes onto a cutting board or serving plate. Using a serrated knife and a light sawing motion, cut each cake into 12 slices each about ¾ inch (2 cm) thick. If not serving the cake right away, tightly wrap the cooled cake in plastic wrap and store at room temperature for up to 5 days.

Serving ideas

Because of its neutral flavor and sturdy texture, pound cake can be served in a variety of ways. You can cut it into slices and spread them with butter and your favorite jam for an indulgent breakfast treat. You can also layer slices with whipped cream and fresh berries for a summertime dessert. For a more formal presentation, bake the batter in a tube pan and sprinkle with confectioners' sugar and candied citrus zest.

Toasted pound cake with butter and jam (top left)
Using a serrated knife, cut the cake into slices ½ inch (12 mm) thick. Toast the slices and spread with butter and jam for breakfast or brunch.

Pound cake with strawberries and cream (left)
Using a serrated knife, cut the pound cake into slices ½ inch (12 mm) thick. Layer the slices with whipped cream (page 77) and strawberries.

Pound cake with candied citrus zest (above)
Bake the cake in a buttered and floured 10-inch (25-cm) tube pan in the lower middle of the oven for 1½ hours. Let cool. Unmold, then sift confectioners' (icing) sugar lightly over the top and sprinkle with candied citrus zest (page 30).

Pound Cake Variations

Once you've mastered the techniques for making Pound Cake (page 49)—creaming butter and sugar, sifting dry ingredients, mixing a simple batter—you can easily expand your cake-making repertory by adding new flavors to the recipe, while keeping the mixing instructions and baking time the same. For example, dry flavorings, such as spices and cocoa powder, are sifted with the flour, and liquid additions, such as coffee, are mixed in with the vanilla extract. Most pound cakes are served plain or with a light dusting of confectioners' sugar, but occasionally a topping of nuts or a simple glaze is added for an extra layer of flavor. Each variation makes 12 servings.

Poppy Seed Pound Cake

The addition of poppy seeds results in a delicious cake with a slightly crunchy texture and somewhat nutty flavor.

Follow the recipe to make Pound Cake. When mixing in the dry ingredients in step 5, mix in ⅓ cup (1½ oz/45 g) poppy seeds after adding half of the dry ingredients. Then add the remaining dry ingredients.

Proceed with the recipe to bake and cool the cakes as directed. Cut the cakes into slices and serve.

> **PASTRY CHEF'S TIP**
> *Regardless of the type of metal, a dark pan absorbs heat more readily than a light-colored one and can cause delicate cakes to overbrown. If you are using a dark pan, watch the cake closely. You may need to reduce the oven temperature or shorten the baking time.*

Ginger Pound Cake

Ginger is added to this cake in three forms: ground, fresh, and crystallized for a mildly spicy flavor.

Follow the recipe to make Pound Cake. When sifting the dry ingredients in step 2, add 4 teaspoons ground ginger and 1 teaspoon ground cinnamon along with the flour, baking powder, and salt. After sifting, mix in ½ cup (2½ oz/75 g) minced crystallized ginger.

When beating in the eggs and vanilla extract in step 4, use only 1 teaspoon vanilla extract (essence) and add 1 tablespoon peeled and finely grated fresh ginger.

Proceed with the recipe to finish the batter and bake and cool the cakes. Cut the cakes into slices and serve.

Lemon Pound Cake

Lemon flavor is layered in this recipe, with the addition of lemon zest to the batter and a tart lemon-juice glaze to the finished cake.

Follow the recipe to make Pound Cake. When creaming the butter and sugar in step 3, beat 1 tablespoon finely grated lemon zest into the mixture.

Proceed with the recipe to finish the batter and bake and cool the cakes.

Next, add 1 cup (4 oz/125 g) sifted confectioners' (icing) sugar and 2 tablespoons fresh lemon juice to a bowl. Using a rubber spatula, stir until the mixture is thick, smooth, and pourable.

Drizzle the glaze over the cakes and let stand for 5 minutes to firm up. Cut the cakes into slices and serve.

Almond Pound Cake

This is another example of layering flavor, with almond paste and almond extract in the batter and sliced almonds scattered on top. The result is a rich-flavored cake with a bit of crunch.

Follow the recipe to make Pound Cake. When creaming the butter and sugar in step 3, add 7 oz (220 g) almond paste to the mixture and mix to incorporate. (You may see a few specks of almond paste after mixing. They will dissolve during further mixing and baking.)

When beating in the eggs and vanilla extract in step 4, use only 2 teaspoons vanilla extract (essence) and add ¾ teaspoon almond extract (essence).

Proceed with the recipe to finish the batter and pour it into the prepared pans. Before baking, sprinkle ¼ cup (1 oz/30 g) sliced (flaked) almonds evenly over the batter in the pans. The almonds will toast in the oven during baking.

Proceed with the recipe to bake and cool the cakes. Cut the cakes into slices and serve.

PASTRY CHEF'S TIP

If you use a lot of vanilla extract (essence), making your own saves money and allows you to control the flavor better. Cut a whole vanilla bean in half lengthwise and place both halves in a glass jar with ¾ cup (6 fl oz/180 ml) vodka. Cap tightly and store in a cool, dark place for 6 months before using.

Chocolate Pound Cake

Cocoa powder in the batter and a glaze made from semisweet chocolate give this cake a double-chocolate flavor.

Follow the recipe to make Pound Cake. When sifting the dry ingredients in step 2, use only 3½ cups (17½ oz/545 g) all-purpose (plain) flour and add ½ cup (1½ oz/45 g) Dutch-process cocoa powder along with the baking powder and salt.

Cream the butter and sugar as directed in step 3. Dissolve 1 teaspoon instant coffee powder in 2 teaspoons water and mix it into the creamed mixture.

Proceed with the recipe to finish the batter and bake and cool the cakes.

Next, cut ½ cup (4 oz/125 g) room-temperature unsalted butter into 8 equal pieces and put into a large heatproof bowl. Add 8 oz (250 g) finely chopped semisweet (plain) chocolate and 1 teaspoon light corn syrup. Place over (not touching) barely simmering water in a saucepan and stir often until the chocolate and butter melt and the mixture is smooth. Remove from the heat and let the glaze cool until slightly thickened, about 5 minutes.

Drizzle the glaze over the cakes, then cut into slices and serve.

Espresso Pound Cake

The addition of instant coffee powder and cocoa powder to the batter and an espresso-based glaze give this cake a strong coffee flavor.

Follow the recipe to make Pound Cake. When sifting the dry ingredients in step 2, use only 3¾ cups (19 oz/590 g) all-purpose (plain) flour and add ¼ cup (¾ oz/20 g) Dutch-process cocoa powder along with the baking powder and salt.

Cream the butter and sugar as directed in step 3. Dissolve 3 tablespoons instant coffee powder in 2 teaspoons water and mix it into the creamed mixture.

Proceed with the recipe to finish the batter and bake and cool the cakes.

Next, place 1 cup (4 oz/125 g) sifted confectioners' (icing) sugar and 2 tablespoons brewed espresso or double-strength coffee into a bowl. Using a rubber spatula, stir until the mixture is thick, smooth, and pourable. Drizzle the glaze over the cakes and let stand for 5 minutes to firm up. Cut the cakes into slices and serve.

Angel Food Cake

Everything about an angel food cake is light. The whipped egg white batter looks like a soft, fluffy marshmallow, and it bakes into a creamy white, delicately textured, stunningly high-rise cake. Since the batter includes no fat, the cake is also a light addition to any calorie-conscious diet.

1 Preheat the oven and prepare the pan

Position a rack in the lower middle of the oven, so the cake will be evenly surrounded with heat, and preheat to 325°F (165°C). Have ready a 10-inch (25-cm) tube pan, preferably with a removable bottom and small feet spaced evenly around the rim (this is sometimes referred to as an angel food cake pan). If the pan does not have feet, have ready a narrow-necked full wine bottle or similar bottle over which the tube of the pan can be slipped while it is cooling. You won't need to grease the pan as you do with most other cakes because any fat, such as butter, can deflate the delicate batter. The batter also needs to adhere to the pan and climb the sides while it bakes.

2 Separate the eggs

If you need help separating eggs, turn to page 36. Take the eggs from the refrigerator (they are easiest to separate when cold). Have ready 2 medium bowls and 1 large mixing bowl. The bowls must be perfectly clean, because even a speck of fat can prevent the whites from reaching the necessary loft when whipped. Working over the first medium bowl, crack 1 egg and pass the yolk back and forth between the shell halves, allowing the white to drop into the bowl. Drop the yolk into the second medium bowl. Transfer the white to the large bowl. Repeat with the remaining 11 eggs. Reserve the yolks for another use, such as Citrus Curd (page 26) or pastry cream (page 128).

3 Sift the dry ingredients

Suspend a fine-mesh sieve over a small bowl and add the flour and ¾ cup (6 oz/185 g) of the sugar. Lightly tap the rim of the sieve to encourage the ingredients to pass into the bowl. This both combines the ingredients and aerates the flour (compacted flour produces a less tender texture, or *crumb*). Set aside. ❯

12 cold large eggs

1 cup (4 oz/125 g) cake (soft-wheat) flour

1¾ cups (14 oz/435 g) granulated sugar

1 teaspoon cream of tartar

¼ teaspoon salt

2 teaspoons vanilla extract (essence)

½ teaspoon almond extract (essence)

MAKES ONE 9¾-INCH (24.5-CM) CAKE,
OR 12 SERVINGS

PASTRY CHEF'S TIP

If you own a copper bowl, you can use it to whip egg whites without the addition of cream of tartar. The copper reacts chemically with the egg protein to produce tall, fluffy, stable whites with a satiny finish.

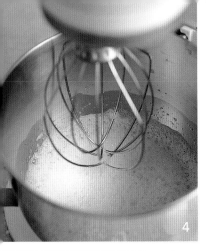

4

5

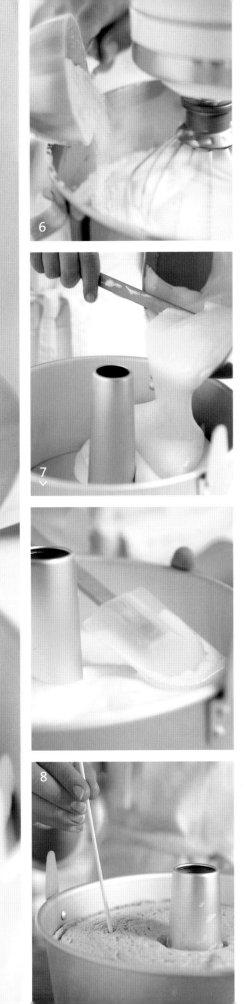

4 Beat the egg whites with the cream of tartar

Add the cream of tartar and salt to the bowl with the egg whites. Fit a stand mixer or a handheld mixer with the whip attachment. Beat on medium speed until opaque white and foamy and the cream of tartar has dissolved, about 1 minute.

5 Beat the egg white mixture to stiff peaks

Increase the speed to medium-high and continue beating, moving the whip around the bowl if using the handheld mixer, until the whites look white, shiny, and smooth and the movement of the whip forms lines in the mixture 2–3 minutes. Stop the mixer and lift the whip. The peaks of the whites should be slightly bent; these are *soft peaks*. Turn the mixer on medium speed and beat in the remaining 1 cup (8 oz/250 g) sugar, at a rate of about 2 tablespoons every 15 seconds, until all the sugar is incorporated. (Remember to move the whip around in the bowl if using a handheld mixer.) The egg whites will be shiny. Stop the mixer and lift the whip. The peaks of the whites should be firm and straight; these are *stiff peaks*. Add the vanilla and almond extracts and beat on medium speed for 1 minute. For more details on beating egg whites, turn to page 37.

6 Mix in the dry ingredients

Reduce the mixer speed to low. Add ½ cup (2½ oz/75 g) of the flour mixture and beat just until incorporated and no streaks are visible. Repeat with the remaining flour mixture in ½-cup additions. When all of the flour mixture has been incorporated, the batter will look soft and fluffy.

7 Transfer the batter to the pan

Using a large rubber spatula, scrape the batter into the prepared pan, then use the spatula to smooth the top. You want to eliminate any large bumps and distribute the batter evenly, but the top does not need to be perfectly smooth.

8 Bake the cake

Bake the cake undisturbed for 40 minutes. If the top looks set—that is, the batter no longer looks wet—and the top is lightly browned, touch it gently. If it feels firm, insert a thin skewer or toothpick near the center of the cake, equidistant from the pan sides and the tube. If it comes out dry, the cake is done. If it comes out wet or with crumbs clinging to it, set the timer for another 5 minutes, continue to bake, and check again. Repeat this process until the cake is done. It will probably take a total of 50 minutes. >

9 Let the cake cool

Using pot holders, carefully remove the cake from the oven. If the pan has feet, invert it onto a wire rack, resting the feet on the wires. If the pan does not have feet, invert the pan onto the neck of a wine bottle. (Angel food cakes need to be cooled upside down because the egg proteins that give the cake its height firm up as the cake cools. If cooled upright, they might collapse and deflate the cake.) Let cool until the cake and the pan are cool to the touch, about 1 hour. Both cooling techniques allow air to circulate around the cake for even cooling and prevent sogginess.

10 Remove the cake from the pan

Remove the pan from the wire rack or bottle and run a thin knife around the sides and center tube of the pan to loosen the cake. Invert a large plate over the pan, and invert the plate and pan together. Lift off the pan. (If your tube pan has a fixed bottom and the cooled cake does not release easily, first carefully loosen the cake from the pan sides with the knife, then use your fingers to reach between the pan and cake and gently pull the cake away from the sides and the bottom of the pan. Rotate the pan and keep working the cake out of the pan until it comes out cleanly.) When the cake has been freed, invert a wire rack over the bottom of the cake, and invert the plate and rack together so the cake is top side up. Lift off the plate. Let the cake cool thoroughly on the wire rack, about 45 minutes.

11 Serve or store the cake

Using your hands, slide the cake onto a serving plate. The cake is quite sturdy when cool, so there is little danger of it breaking or crumbling in transport. Using a serrated knife and a light sawing motion, cut the cake into 12 wedges. If not serving the cake right away, you can wrap the cooled cake or any leftover cake in plastic wrap and store at room temperature for up to 3 days.

PASTRY CHEF'S TIP

Cream of tartar is used in angel food cakes primarily to stabilize the egg whites, but it also lowers the pH of the batter, resulting in a whiter crumb.

Serving ideas

You can dress up Angel Food Cake with one of these three simple ideas: Top the cake slices with sugared flowers, for a pretty presentation with a touch of sweetness. For chocolate aficionados, drizzle each slice with ganache and top with a fresh mint sprig. Or, serve the slices with berries tossed with sugar for added color and texture. Delicate clear-glass dessert plates are perfect for serving.

Angel food cake with sugared flowers (top left)
Place a few sugared flowers (page 31) on top of each cake slice.

Angel food cake with chocolate and mint (left)
Select 12 small fresh mint sprigs. Drizzle 1–2 tablespoons warm ganache (page 28) over each slice, then place a mint sprig on top.

Angel food cake with fresh berries (above)
Have ready 2 cups (8 oz/250 g) mixed berries. If using strawberries, remove the hulls and halve or quarter them. Toss the berries in ¼ cup (2 oz/60 g) sugar and let *macerate*, or soak, for about 15 minutes to draw out the juices. Spoon the berries and their juices alongside or on top of each cake slice.

Apple Cake

Cinnamon sugar plays a dual role in this tender-crumbed, wonderfully moist cake. It forms sweet swirls of cinnamon inside the cake, and it bakes into a crunchy crown on top. The apples are shredded, rather than chopped, which ensures that they soften fully by the time the cake is finished baking.

1 Preheat the oven and prepare the pan
Position a rack in the lower middle of the oven, so the cake will be evenly surrounded with heat, and preheat to 350°F (180°C). Butter a 10-inch (25-cm) fixed-bottom tube pan and sprinkle it lightly with flour, then tap out the extra flour. For more details on buttering and flouring pans, turn to page 34.

2 Make the cinnamon sugar
In a small bowl, stir together the sugar and the cinnamon until no white streaks of sugar are visible. Set aside.

3 Sift the dry ingredients
Suspend a fine-mesh sieve over a small bowl and add the flour, baking powder, baking soda, and salt. Lightly tap the rim of the sieve to encourage the ingredients to pass into the bowl. This both combines the ingredients and aerates the flour (compacted flour produces a less tender texture, or *crumb*). Set the bowl aside.

4 Peel and shred the apples
Using a vegetable peeler, remove the skin from each apple. Using a box grater-shredder held over a sheet of waxed paper, repeatedly draw one side of a peeled apple against the large shredding holes. Stop shredding when you reach the core and seeds, rotate the apple to another side, and shred again. Continue rotating and shredding until only the core is left. Spoon the shredded apple into a glass measuring cup. Shred the remaining apple(s) in the same way until you have 2 cups (8 oz/250 g). Transfer the shredded apples to a small bowl, and stir in about half of the cinnamon sugar. Set aside for 15 minutes to let the apples absorb the flavor. As the shredded apples stand, their juices will be slowly released into the bowl.

5 Drain the apples
Suspend a fine-mesh sieve over a bowl and pour the apple mixture into it. Do not press on the apples, but let any juice drain off into the bowl. (Draining the apples prevents excessive moisture from being added to the batter, which could cause the cake to fail to rise properly when baked.) Discard the juice and set the shredded apples aside.

Unsalted butter and flour for preparing the pan

For the cinnamon sugar

½ cup (4 oz/125 g) granulated sugar

1 tablespoon ground cinnamon

2¾ cups (11 oz/345 g) cake (soft-wheat) flour

1 teaspoon baking powder

½ teaspoon baking soda (bicarbonate of soda)

½ teaspoon salt

3 medium or 2 large Granny Smith apples, about 1½ lb (750 g) total weight

3 large eggs

2 cups (1 lb/500 g) granulated sugar

2 teaspoons vanilla extract (essence)

1 cup (8 fl oz/250 ml) canola oil or corn oil

1 cup (8 oz/250 g) sour cream

MAKES ONE 10-INCH (25-CM) TUBE CAKE, OR 12–16 SERVINGS

PASTRY CHEF'S TIP
Salt has many roles in cooking. Among them is bringing out the flavors in sweet baked goods. Here, salt helps to intensify the apple flavor in the cake.

6 Beat the eggs with the sugar

In a large mixing bowl or the bowl of a stand mixer, combine the eggs and the sugar. Fit the handheld mixer with the twin beaters or the stand mixer with the paddle attachment. Beat the mixture on medium-high speed until it thickens and the color lightens slightly, about 2 minutes. If using a handheld mixer, move the beaters around in the bowl to make sure every bit is well beaten. Stop the mixer occasionally and use a rubber spatula to scrape down any batter from the sides of the bowl into the remaining ingredients.

7 Finish the batter

Reduce the speed to low and beat in the vanilla extract. Slowly pour in the oil, mixing just until it is blended into the batter, about 1 minute. Do not add the oil too quickly, or it might splash out of the bowl. Add the dry ingredients in 2 equal additions, and beat after each addition just until incorporated. Add the sour cream and continue mixing just until no white streaks remain. Finally, add the shredded apples and mix just until evenly distributed throughout the batter. The batter will thin slightly when the apples are added.

8 Bake the cake

Pour about two-thirds of the batter into the prepared pan, turning the pan as you pour so the batter fills it evenly. Sprinkle half of the remaining cinnamon sugar evenly over the batter in the pan (this will form an interesting swirl in the middle of each cake slice). Pour the remaining batter over the cinnamon sugar, using the spatula to scrape out every last bit from the bowl. The batter may not cover the cinnamon sugar completely. Sprinkle the remaining cinnamon sugar evenly over the top. Bake undisturbed for 50 minutes. If the cake looks set—that is, the batter no longer looks liquid and the top is lightly browned—touch the top gently. If it feels firm, insert a thin skewer or toothpick in the center. If it comes out dry, the cake is done. If it comes out wet or with crumbs clinging to it, set the timer for another 5 minutes, continue to bake, and check again. Repeat this process until the cake is done. It will probably take no longer than 1 hour.

9 Let the cake cool

Using pot holders, carefully transfer the cake to a wire rack. Let cool in the pan for 20 minutes. Run a thin knife along the inside edge of the pan and the tube to loosen the cake, keeping the knife pressed against the pan sides. Invert a plate on top of the cake and invert together. The cake will release from the pan. Lift off the pan. Invert another wire rack on the cake and invert the racks together so the cake is top side up. Lift off the top rack. Let the cake cool completely on the rack, about 1½ hours.

10 Serve or store the cake

Carefully slide the cake onto a serving plate. Using a serrated knife and a light sawing motion, cut the cake into 12–16 wedges. Or, tightly wrap the cooled cake with plastic wrap and store at room temperature for up to 4 days.

Apple Cake Variations

Now that you've practiced the skills you need to make Apple Cake on page 63—sifting dry ingredients, layering a fruit-infused batter with cinnamon sugar—you can make a trio of similar cakes by changing just a few ingredients. The Spice Cake leaves out the apples but calls for a quartet of winter spices, giving the cake an intriguing aromatic flavor. Or, you can replace the apples with other fruits. Bananas, for example, blend well with the spices and give the cake a softer texture. Dried figs, which are sweeter and denser than fresh ones, result in a cake with a chewier texture and a distinctive richness. Each variation makes 12–16 servings.

Spice Cake

A mixture of fragrant spices replaces the apples in this flavorful cake, which is perfect for teatime.

Follow the recipe for Apple Cake. When making the cinnamon sugar in step 2, use 6 tablespoons (3 oz/90 g) sugar and 1½ teaspoons ground cinnamon.

When sifting the dry ingredients in step 3, add 1 teaspoon ground cinnamon, 1 teaspoon ground ginger, ½ teaspoon freshly grated nutmeg, and ½ teaspoon ground cloves to the flour, baking powder, baking soda (bicarbonate of soda), and salt.

Proceed with the recipe starting at step 6, omitting the shredded apples, and then bake, cool, and serve the cake as directed.

Banana Cake

In this variation, bananas replace the apples. Make sure they are soft and ripe and free of any green areas on the peel.

Follow the recipe for Apple Cake. When making the cinnamon sugar in step 2, use ¼ cup (2 oz/60 g) sugar and 1 teaspoon ground cinnamon.

Next, peel 4 ripe bananas and break each one into 3 or 4 pieces. Add the pieces to a bowl and use a fork to mash them.

Proceed with the recipe starting at step 6, substituting the bananas for the apples. Bake, cool, and serve the cake as directed.

Fig Cake

Here, dried figs are substituted for the apples, giving the cake additional sweetness.

Follow the recipe for Apple Cake. When making the cinnamon sugar in step 2, use 6 tablespoons (3 oz/90 g) sugar and 1½ teaspoons ground cinnamon.

Next, mix 2 cups (8 oz/250 g) dried Black Mission or Calimyrna fig pieces (½-inch/ 12-mm pieces) with the cinnamon sugar in a small bowl.

Proceed with the recipe starting at step 6, substituting the figs and any loose sugar that remains in the bowl for the apples. Bake, cool, and serve the cake as directed.

Pineapple Upside-Down Cake

Here, the signature sticky topping of brown sugar and fruit bakes right along with a standard butter cake. Once the cake is out of the oven, all you have to do is wait for it to cool and it is ready to serve with no additional filling or frosting. As the cake bakes, the sweetness of the fruit topping intensifies, becoming almost like candy.

1 **Preheat the oven and prepare the cake pan**
Position a rack in the middle of the oven and preheat to 350°F (180°C). Butter a 9-inch (23-cm) round layer cake pan. Line the bottom with parchment (baking) paper cut to fit and then butter the parchment paper (you do not need to flour the pan). For more details on preparing pans, turn to page 34.

2 **Prepare the pineapple**
Lay the pineapple on its side on a cutting board. Using a serrated knife, cut off the green top and cut a thin slice from the bottom. Stand the fruit upright and cut away the dark brown peel in strips, using vertical strokes and rotating the fruit as each strip of peel is removed. Once again lay the pineapple on its side. Switch to a paring knife and cut away the brown "eyes" by cutting along either side of them at an angle and working in a spiral pattern. Use the serrated knife to cut the fruit crosswise into slices ½ inch (12 mm) thick. Using the paring knife, cut out the hard core at the center of each slice and discard. Set the slices aside.

3 **Make the topping**
In a saucepan over medium heat, combine the butter, honey, and brown sugar. Heat, stirring constantly with a heatproof spatula, until the butter and brown sugar melt and the mixture is smooth, about 4 minutes. Pour the mixture into the prepared cake pan, using the spatula to remove every last bit from the saucepan. Pick up the cake pan and tilt it slightly to cover the bottom evenly with the topping. Put as many pineapple slices as will fit snugly around the edge of the pan, then place 1 slice in the center. Reserve any remaining pineapple for another use. Put 1 dried cherry in the center of each pineapple slice.

4 **Sift the dry ingredients**
Suspend a fine-mesh sieve over a small bowl and add the flour, baking powder, and salt. Lightly tap the rim of the sieve to encourage the ingredients to pass into the bowl. This both combines the ingredients and aerates the flour (compacted flour produces a less tender texture, or *crumb*). Set the bowl aside.

5 **Cream the butter and sugar**
In the bowl of a stand mixer, or a large mixing bowl, combine the butter and granulated sugar. Fit a stand mixer with the paddle attachment or a handheld mixer with the twin beaters. Beat on medium speed until the mixture is light and airy, about 2 minutes. If using a handheld mixer, move the beaters around in the bowl to beat the mixture evenly. Scrape the sides of the bowl occasionally with a rubber spatula. For more details on creaming butter, turn to page 38. >

Unsalted butter for preparing the pan

For the topping

1 pineapple

4 tablespoons (2 oz/60 g) unsalted butter, cut into 4 equal pieces

2 tablespoons honey

1 cup (7 oz/220 g) firmly packed light brown sugar

7–9 dried cherries

For the Classic Butter Cake

1¼ cups (5 oz/155 g) plus 2 tablespoons cake (soft-wheat) flour

1 teaspoon baking powder

⅛ teaspoon salt

½ cup (4 oz/125 g) unsalted butter, at room temperature

1 cup (8 oz/250 g) granulated sugar

2 large eggs, at room temperature

1 teaspoon vanilla extract (essence)

½ cup (4 fl oz/125 ml) whole milk, at room temperature

MAKES ONE 9-INCH (23-CM) CAKE, OR 8 SERVINGS

6 Beat in the eggs and vanilla extract

Add the eggs to the butter mixture one at a time, beating for 1 minute after each addition to incorporate each egg fully. Stop the mixer occasionally and use a rubber spatula to scrape any batter from the sides of the bowl into the remaining mixture. After all of the eggs have been added, add the vanilla extract and beat for 1 minute longer to mix fully.

7 Finish the batter

Reduce the mixer speed to low. Add one-third of the dry ingredients and mix until incorporated. Next, add one-half of the milk and mix until incorporated. Continue alternately adding the ingredients in the same manner, ending with the last third of the dry ingredients. The order is important, especially if the milk is not at room temperature. When you add cold milk, the batter will look curdled, because any cold ingredient can firm up bits of the butter. But once the dry ingredients are added, the batter loses its curdled look and becomes smooth. This makes ending with a measure of dry ingredients critical.

8 Transfer the batter to the topping-lined pan

Pour the batter into the pan, being careful not to disturb the pineapple topping. Use the spatula to scrape every last bit of batter from the bowl, then gently smooth the top to distribute the batter evenly. It does not need to be perfectly smooth; the top of the cake becomes smooth during baking.

9 Bake the cake

Bake undisturbed for 50 minutes. If it looks set and the top is lightly browned, insert a thin skewer or toothpick in the center, being careful to touch only the cake and not the topping. If it comes out dry, the cake is done. If it comes out wet or with crumbs clinging to it, set the timer for another 5 minutes, continue to bake, and check again. Repeat until the cake is done. It will probably take a total of 55 minutes. Using pot holders, transfer the cake to a wire rack. Let cool in the pan for 10 minutes.

10 Unmold and cool the cake

Run a thin knife along the inside edge of the pan to loosen the cake, keeping the knife pressed against the pan sides. Invert a wire rack on top of the cake and invert the pan and rack together. The cake will release from the pan. Lift off the pan, then peel off the parchment and replace any topping that sticks to the paper. Discard the parchment. Let the cake cool to room temperature, about 1 hour.

11 Serve or store the cake

Carefully slide the cake onto a serving plate. Using a serrated knife and a light sawing motion, cut the cake into 8 wedges. Or, tightly wrap the cooled cake with plastic wrap and store at room temperature for up to 2 days.

Upside-Down Cake Variations

In making the Pineapple Upside-Down Cake on page 67, you learned how to cook pineapple in butter, honey, and brown sugar, an important technique called *caramelizing*. The batter is then poured over the pineapple, so that the fruit bakes on the bottom of the pan. When the cake comes out of the oven, it is turned upside down to serve, which is how it got its name. Once you have mastered this cake and fully understand its components, you will have the confidence to make it with other fruits. The three variations below substitute mango, apple, or pear for the pineapple, while all the other ingredients and techniques remain the same. Each variation makes 8 servings.

Mango Upside-Down Cake

Look for ripe but firm mangoes with a reddish cast for the best result.

Preheat the oven and prepare the pan as directed.

Next, using a small, sharp knife, peel away the skin from 2 mangoes. Still using the knife and working with 1 mango at a time, remove the fruit from the large, flat pit, starting at the stem end and cutting a long, vertical wedge about ½ inch (12 mm) thick. Once you cut the first wedge, lay the mango on its side on a paper towel (to keep it from slipping), and cut the remaining flesh into wedges the same way. Repeat with the remaining mango. You will need 24–26 wedges to fill the pan.

Proceed with the recipe to make the topping. Beginning at the edge of the pan, neatly arrange the mango wedges, overlapping them slightly, over the topping in the pan. You will have a small circle in the center that is not covered. Arrange 4 additional mango wedges in the center.

Continue with the recipe to bake, unmold, and serve or store the cake.

Apple Upside-Down Cake

Choose apples that are good for baking, such as Granny Smith or pippin.

Preheat the oven and prepare the pan as directed.

Next, use a vegetable peeler to remove the skins from 2 apples. Hold 1 apple, stem side up, on a cutting board. Using a chef's knife and positioning it about ¼ inch (6 mm) from the stem indentation, cut away half of the apple. Positioning the knife to leave the core behind, cut half of what is left of the apple away from the core. Finally, cut the last section of apple away from the core. You will have 3 large pieces of apple with flat sides. If any seeds or core remain in the apple pieces, use a small knife to remove them. Place each section, flat side down, on the cutting board and cut it into slices ⅓ inch (9 mm) thick. Repeat with the remaining apple. You will need 32–34 slices to fill the pan.

Proceed with the recipe to make the topping. Beginning at the edge of the pan, neatly arrange the apple slices, overlapping them slightly, over the topping mixture in the pan. Arrange a second smaller circle in the center.

Continue with the recipe to bake, unmold, and serve or store the cake.

Pear Upside-Down Cake

Choose pears that are good for baking, such as Anjou or Bosc.

Preheat the oven and prepare the pan as directed.

Next, use a vegetable peeler to remove the skins from 2 pears. Hold 1 pear, stem side up, on a cutting board. Using a chef's knife and positioning it about ¼ inch (6 mm) from the stem indentation, cut away half of the pear. Positioning the knife to leave the core behind, cut half of what is left of the pear away from the core. Finally, cut the last section of pear away from the core. You will have 3 large pieces of pear with flat sides. If any seeds or core remain in the pear pieces, use a small knife to remove them. Place each section, flat side down, on the cutting board and cut it into slices ¼ inch (6 mm) thick. Repeat with the remaining pear. You will need 32–34 slices to fill the pan.

Proceed with the recipe to make the topping. Beginning at the edge of the pan, neatly arrange the pear slices, overlapping them slightly, over the topping mixture in the pan. Arrange a second smaller circle in the center.

Continue with the recipe to bake, unmold, and serve or store the cake.

Carrot Cake

The batter in this beloved classic is easy to mix, and the texture of the finished cake is consistently moist—thanks to the combination of oil, carrots, and crushed pineapple. The bright white frosting is smooth, creamy, and rich, qualities it owes to the use of butter and cream cheese.

Unsalted butter and flour for preparing the pans

For the cake

2 cups (10 oz/315 g) all-purpose (plain) flour

1½ teaspoons baking soda (bicarbonate of soda)

1 teaspoon ground cinnamon

½ teaspoon salt

4 large eggs

2 cups (1 lb/500 g) granulated sugar

1 teaspoon vanilla extract (essence)

1 cup (8 fl oz/250 ml) canola oil or corn oil

2 cups (6 oz/185 g) finely grated carrots (from 5 or 6 carrots)

1 can (8 oz/250 g) crushed pineapple in its own juice, well drained

1 cup (4 oz/125 g) finely chopped walnuts

For the cream cheese frosting

½ lb (250 g) cream cheese, at room temperature

¾ cup (6 oz/185 g) unsalted butter, at room temperature

2 teaspoons vanilla extract (essence)

4 cups (1 lb/500 g) confectioners' (icing) sugar

For the topping

1 cup (4 oz/125 g) coarsely chopped walnuts

MAKES ONE 9-INCH (23-CM) CAKE,
OR 12 SERVINGS

1 Preheat the oven and prepare the pans
Position a rack in the lower middle of the oven and preheat to 350°F (180°C). Butter two 9-inch (23-cm) round layer cake pans. Line the pans with parchment (baking) paper. Butter the paper, sprinkle it lightly with flour, and then tap out the excess flour. For more details on preparing pans, turn to page 34.

2 Mix the cake batter
Sift the flour, baking soda, cinnamon, and salt through a fine-mesh sieve placed over a medium bowl. Set aside. In the bowl of a stand mixer or a large mixing bowl, combine the eggs and granulated sugar. Fit a stand mixer with the paddle attachment or a handheld mixer with the twin beaters. Beat the mixture on medium-high speed until it thickens and the color lightens slightly, about 2 minutes. Reduce the speed to low and beat in the vanilla extract. Slowly pour in the oil, mixing just until blended, about 1 minute. Add the flour mixture and mix just until no white streaks are visible. Add the carrots, pineapple, and finely chopped walnuts and mix until evenly distributed, 1–2 minutes.

3 Bake and cool the layers
Pour the batter into the prepared pans, dividing it evenly and lightly smoothing the tops. Bake until the tops look evenly browned, feel firm to the touch, and a thin skewer or toothpick inserted in the center comes out dry, 30–35 minutes. Using pot holders, transfer the cakes to wire racks and let cool for 20 minutes. Working with 1 pan at a time, run a thin knife along the inside of the pan. Invert a wire rack on the pan and invert together. Lift off the pan and peel off the parchment. Invert another wire rack on the cake and invert the racks together, so the cake is top side up. Lift off the top rack. Let the cake cool completely on the rack, about 45 minutes. Repeat with the second cake layer.

4 Frost and serve the cake
Use the paddle attachment on a stand mixer or the twin beaters on a handheld mixer to mix the cream cheese, butter, and vanilla extract on medium speed until smooth and creamy, about 1 minute. Reduce the speed to low and mix in the confectioners' sugar until smooth. Transfer 1 cake layer to a plate. Using an icing spatula, spread about one-half of the frosting evenly over the cake. Center the second layer on top. Wipe the spatula clean, then spread about one-fourth of the frosting in a thin layer over the top and sides of the cake. Wipe the spatula clean again, and spread the remaining frosting in a smooth layer over the top and sides of the cake. For details on frosting cakes, turn to page 43. Top the cake with the coarsely chopped walnuts. Cut the cake into 12 wedges and serve right away.

Brown-Butter Hazelnut Cakes

These bite-sized cakes, called *financiers* in France, are moist and chewy on the inside and crusty and golden on the outside. They carry layers of nutty flavor, from the toasted hazelnuts and the nutlike flavor of the brown butter. Only a small amount of flour is used. Instead, the structure comes mostly from ground hazelnuts.

1 **Preheat the oven and prepare the pans**
Position a rack in the middle of the oven and preheat to 350°F (180°C). Line 24 mini-muffin cups (each 2 inches/5 cm wide and ¾ inch/2 cm deep) with paper liners.

2 **Toast and peel the hazelnuts**
Place the nuts on a small rimmed baking sheet and toast in the preheated oven, stirring occasionally, until fragrant and the color deepens, 15–20 minutes. After the warm nuts have cooled to the touch, rub them firmly with a kitchen towel and use your fingers to peel away as much of the skin as you can.

3 **Prepare the dry ingredients**
Sift the flour through a fine-mesh sieve placed over a large bowl. Stir in the granulated sugar and set aside. In a food processor, combine the hazelnuts and the ⅔ cup confectioners' sugar. Pulse to chop the nuts coarsely, then process until finely ground, about 1 minute. Stir together the nut and flour mixtures; set aside.

4 **Make the brown butter and mix the batter**
Place a small frying pan over medium heat and add the butter. The butter will spatter for about the first 5 minutes so be careful to avoid burns. When the spattering stops, a light brown foam will form at the edge of the pan and the butter will begin to brown, emitting a nutty aroma. Watch carefully now, and when you see some brown flecks on the pan bottom, the butter is ready; this should take about 7 minutes total. Immediately remove from the heat. Using a large heatproof spatula, scrape the warm butter into the flour-nut mixture and stir until the dry ingredients are moistened. Pour in about half of the egg whites and stir until incorporated. Add the remaining egg whites and stir until smooth.

5 **Bake and cool the cakes**
Fill each prepared muffin cup with a level tablespoon of batter. Wipe off any spills that drip on the pan. Bake until they look set, are firm to the touch, and a thin skewer or toothpick inserted in the center comes out clean, 14–18 minutes. Let cool in the pans for 10 minutes. Invert a wire rack on top of a pan and invert together. The cakes will release from the pan. Turn the cakes top side up on the rack. Repeat the unmolding with the second pan and let cool completely.

6 **Serve the cakes**
Put the 2 tablespoons confectioners' sugar in the fine-mesh sieve and lightly dust the tops of the cakes. Serve right away.

⅔ cup (3 oz/90 g) hazelnuts (filberts) with skins

½ cup (2 oz/60 g) cake (soft-wheat) flour

½ cup (4 oz/125 g) granulated sugar

⅔ cup (2½ oz/75 g) plus 2 tablespoons confectioners' (icing) sugar

½ cup (4 oz/125 g) unsalted butter, cut into 8 equal pieces

3 large egg whites, lightly beaten

MAKES 24 SERVINGS

MAKE-AHEAD TIP
Once the cakes have cooled completely, you can wrap them tightly in plastic wrap and store at room temperature for up to 2 days. Dust the tops with confectioners' sugar just before serving.

Orange Chiffon Cake

The secret to this tall, moist, light cake is the careful folding of two fluffy mixtures. You can also prepare this recipe with a stand mixer, use the paddle attachment to make the batter. Be sure the bowl you use to whip the egg whites is spotlessly clean and grease free.

For the cake

2¼ cups (9 oz/280 g) cake (soft-wheat) flour

1½ cups (12 oz/375 g) granulated sugar

1½ teaspoons baking powder

½ teaspoon salt

½ cup (4 fl oz/125 ml) canola oil

7 cold large eggs, separated (page 36)

½ cup (4 fl oz/125 ml) fresh orange juice

¼ cup (2 fl oz/60 ml) water

2 teaspoons finely grated orange zest (page 35)

1 teaspoon vanilla extract (essence)

½ teaspoon cream of tartar

For the glaze

1 cup (4 oz/125 g) confectioners' (icing) sugar, sifted

2 tablespoons unsalted butter, melted

2½–3 tablespoons fresh orange juice

MAKES ONE 10-INCH (25-CM) CAKE, OR 12 SERVINGS

PASTRY CHEF'S TIP
To maximize the amount of juice extracted from an orange, loosen the flesh from the skin before squeezing: using your palm, gently roll the orange over a firm, flat surface.

1 **Preheat the oven and prepare the pan**
Position a rack in the lower middle of the oven and preheat to 325°F (165°C). Have ready an ungreased 10-inch (25-cm) tube pan with a fixed bottom and small feet spaced evenly around the rim.

2 **Make the batter**
Sift the flour, 1 cup (8 oz/250 g) of the granulated sugar, the baking powder, and the salt through a fine-mesh sieve placed over a large mixing bowl. Using a large spoon, make a well in the center, and add the oil, egg yolks, orange juice, water, orange zest, and vanilla extract. Fit a handheld mixer with the twin beaters. Beat the mixture until well blended, smooth, and thick, about 3 minutes.

3 **Lighten the batter with egg whites**
Combine the egg whites and cream of tartar in a large, clean bowl. Fit the mixer with the whip attachment, then beat the mixture on medium speed until foamy, about 1 minute. Increase the speed to medium-high and continue beating until the whites form *soft peaks* when you lift the whip, 2–3 minutes. Gradually beat in the remaining ½ cup (4 oz/125 g) sugar, then beat for 1 minute longer until shiny and stiff. Gently fold about one-third of the beaten whites into the beaten yolk mixture. Spoon the remaining egg whites on top and fold in until no white streaks are visible. For more details on whipping egg whites and folding, turn to pages 37 and 39.

4 **Bake and cool the cake**
Using the spatula, transfer the batter to the prepared pan and smooth the top. Bake until the top is lightly browned, feels firm to the touch, and a thin skewer or toothpick inserted near the center comes out dry, 55–60 minutes. Using pot holders, invert the pan and stand it on its feet on a wire rack. Let cool until the cake is cool to the touch, about 1 hour. Run a thin knife around the sides and center tube of the pan to loosen the cake, then invert onto a plate. Invert a wire rack over the cake and invert the plate and rack together, so the cake is top side up on the rack. Remove the plate. Let cool completely, about 45 minutes.

5 **Glaze and serve the cake**
In a bowl, using a spoon, stir together the confectioners' sugar, melted butter, and 2½ tablespoons of the orange juice until a thick, smooth glaze forms, adding additional juice if needed to achieve a pourable consistency. Use the spoon to drizzle the glaze over the cooled cake, letting it drip down the sides. Slide the cake onto a serving plate, cut into 12 wedges, and serve right away.

Flourless Chocolate Cake

Don't be fooled by the small size of this cake. It may measure only 1½ inches (4 cm) high, but every bite is packed with intense chocolate flavor. Its texture is similar to a dense soufflé with a soft, smooth center, but it's easier to make. A spoonful of snowy white whipped cream looks particularly appealing against the deep brown cake.

1 **Preheat the oven and prepare the pan**
Position a rack in the middle of the oven and preheat to 375°F (190°C). Butter an 8-inch (20-cm) springform pan. Line the bottom with parchment (baking) paper cut to fit. Butter the paper, sprinkle it lightly with flour, then tap out the excess flour. For more details on preparing the pan, turn to page 34.

2 **Make the chocolate cake base**
Combine the chocolate and butter in a large heatproof bowl and melt over barely simmering water. (If you need help melting chocolate, turn to page 40.) Set aside to cool slightly, about 5 minutes. In a small bowl, combine the egg yolks, dissolved coffee, and vanilla extract and whisk just until blended. Pour the yolk mixture over the cooled chocolate and whisk until no streaks of egg are visible.

3 **Whip the egg whites and fold them into the cake base**
In the bowl of a stand mixer or a large, clean mixing bowl, combine the egg whites and cream of tartar. Fit a stand mixer or handheld mixer with the whip attachment. Beat on medium speed until foamy and the cream of tartar dissolves, about 1 minute. Increase the speed to medium-high and continue beating until the whites form *soft peaks*, 2–3 minutes. Add the granulated sugar in 2 batches, beating for 15 seconds after each addition. Then beat for 1 minute longer; the whites should be shiny and stiff. Using a rubber spatula, gently fold about one-third of the beaten egg whites into the chocolate mixture. Spoon the remaining whites on top and fold in until no white streaks remain. For more details on whipping egg whites and folding, turn to pages 37 and 39.

4 **Bake and cool the cake**
Pour the batter into the prepared pan and smooth the top. Bake until the cake puffs up, the top looks firm, and the middle jiggles only very slightly when the pan is gently shaken, 19–23 minutes. Transfer to a wire rack and let cool in the pan for 30 minutes. The cake will sink slightly in the middle. Run a thin knife along the inside edge of the pan to loosen the cake, then release the sides and lift them off. Let the cake cool completely, about 1 hour longer.

5 **Serve the cake**
Use a thin knife to loosen the cake from the pan bottom. Then, using 2 wide metal spatulas, slide the cake onto a serving plate. Have ready a tall glass filled with hot water and a large, sharp knife. Cut the cake into 8 wedges, dipping the knife in the water and wiping it clean before each cut. Use a wide metal spatula to transfer the wedges to individual plates.

Unsalted butter and flour for preparing the pan

8 oz (250 g) semisweet (plain) chocolate, finely chopped (page 40)

½ cup (4 oz/125 g) unsalted butter, cut into 8 equal pieces

4 cold large eggs, separated (page 36)

1 teaspoon instant coffee dissolved in 2 teaspoons water

1 teaspoon vanilla extract (essence)

¼ teaspoon cream of tartar

¼ cup (2 oz/60 g) granulated sugar

MAKES ONE 8-INCH (20-CM) CAKE, OR 8 SERVINGS

PASTRY CHEF'S TIP
Lightly sweetened whipped cream is the perfect foil for slices of dense chocolate cake such as this. It can also dress up slices of Pound Cake (page 49). Use the whip attachment of a mixer to beat together 1 cup (8 fl oz/250 ml) cold heavy (double) cream, 2 tablespoons confectioners' (icing) sugar, and 1 teaspoon vanilla extract (essence) until soft peaks form.

4

Cake Layers
& Sheet Cakes

Before you can advance to making elaborate cakes, you need
to learn how to bake the cake layers and sheet cakes that
form their foundation. In this chapter, you'll find examples
of both foam cakes—sponge cake and génoise—and
butter cakes—classic yellow cake and devil's food cake—
that you can pair with fillings and frostings to make
multilayered cakes and filled cake rolls.

Sponge Cake Layers

Light, airy sponge cake layers obtain their height from vigorously beaten eggs, which form a network of air bubbles that rise in the heat of the oven. After baking and cooling, these layers—either vanilla or chocolate—can be paired with a variety of fillings and frostings to make appealing desserts.

1 Preheat the oven and prepare the pans
Position a rack in the middle of the oven, so the cakes will be evenly surrounded with heat, and preheat to 350°F (180°C). Place a small amount of butter on a piece of waxed paper and spread the butter evenly over the bottom and sides of two 9-inch (23-cm) round layer cake pans. Line the bottoms with parchment (baking) paper, butter the paper, then sprinkle lightly with flour. Tap out the excess flour. For more details on preparing cake pans, turn to page 34.

2 Sift the dry ingredients
Suspend a fine-mesh sieve over a small bowl. If making vanilla sponge cake, add the flour and salt. If making chocolate sponge cake, add the flour, cocoa powder, coffee powder, and salt. Lightly tap the rim of the sieve to encourage the ingredients to pass into the bowl. This both combines the ingredients and aerates the flour (compacted flour produces a less tender texture, or *crumb*). Set aside.

3 Beat the egg yolks with half the sugar
In the bowl of a stand mixer or a large mixing bowl, combine the egg yolks and ½ cup (4 oz/125 g) of the granulated sugar. Fit the stand mixer with the paddle attachment or a handheld mixer with the twin beaters. Beat on medium-high speed until thickened, pale yellow, and the batter falls back on itself like a ribbon when the beater is lifted, about 3 minutes. Stop the mixer occasionally and, using a rubber spatula, scrape down the bowl sides. (For more details on beating eggs to the ribbon stage, turn to page 37.) Add the vanilla extract and beat until combined. If using the stand mixer, scrape the yolk mixture into a large bowl. Wash and dry the mixer bowl thoroughly. ›

Unsalted butter and flour for preparing the pans

For vanilla cake layers

1 cup (4 oz/125 g) cake (soft-wheat) flour

Pinch of salt

6 large eggs, separated (page 36), at room temperature

1 cup (8 oz/250 g) granulated sugar

1 teaspoon vanilla extract (essence)

For chocolate cake layers

¾ cup (3 oz/90 g) cake (soft-wheat) flour

¼ cup (¾ oz/20 g) Dutch-process cocoa powder

½ teaspoon instant coffee powder

⅛ teaspoon salt

6 large eggs, separated (page 36), at room temperature

1 cup (8 oz/250 g) granulated sugar

1 teaspoon vanilla extract (essence)

MAKES TWO 9-INCH (23-CM) CAKE LAYERS

RECOMMENDED USES
Classic Birthday Cake (page 105), Banana Layer Cake (page 111), and Black Forest Cake (page 111).

4>>

4 Beat the egg whites with the remaining sugar

To the clean stand mixer bowl or a large mixing bowl, add the egg whites. Fit the mixer with the whip attachment. Beat on medium speed until foamy, about 1 minute. Increase the speed to medium-high and continue beating, moving the whip around the bowl if necessary, until the whites look shiny and smooth and hold slightly bent peaks—*soft peaks*—when you stop the mixer and lift the whip, 2–3 minutes. Turn the mixer on medium speed and beat in the remaining ½ cup sugar at a rate of about 2 tablespoons every 15 seconds. After all of the sugar has been incorporated, beat the whites for 1 minute longer. When you stop the mixer and lift the whip, the peaks will be firm and straight; these are *stiff peaks*. For more details on beating egg whites, turn to page 37.

5 Fold the egg whites into the egg yolks

Using a rubber spatula, pile about one-third of the egg whites on top of the yolk mixture. Then, using the spatula, fold the mixtures together: Slice down through the center to the bottom of the bowl, pull the spatula to the side, and, keeping the flat side of the spatula against the side of the bowl, bring the spatula up and over the top of the egg whites, bringing some of the yolk mixture with it. Rotate the bowl a quarter turn and repeat the folding action until no white streaks remain. This first addition will lighten the batter. Now, pile the remaining egg whites on top of the mixture and fold them in using the same technique. If you need help with the folding technique, turn to page 39.

6 Fold in the flour mixture

Still using the spatula, fold in the flour mixture in 4 additions: Sprinkle about one-fourth of the flour mixture over the egg mixture, then, using the same technique as above, fold in the mixture just until no streaks of flour (or cocoa powder) are visible. Repeat with the remaining flour mixture. (Adding the dry ingredients in small amounts prevents their weight from deflating the egg mixture.) The batter will be light and foamy. ⟩

PASTRY CHEF'S TIP

It is important to beat egg whites in a spotlessly clean and dry bowl. Any trace of grease, fat, or water will prevent them from expanding to their full volume. If your egg whites do not expand in volume after a few minutes of beating, discard them and start over with a clean, dry bowl and fresh egg whites.

7 Bake the cakes

Pour the batter into the prepared pans, dividing it evenly. Use the spatula to scrape every last bit from the bowl and then to smooth the surface lightly. Bake the cakes undisturbed for 18 minutes. If the cakes look set and the surface is lightly browned, touch the tops gently. If they feel firm, insert a thin skewer or toothpick in the centers. If it comes out dry, the cakes are done. If it comes out wet or with crumbs clinging to it, set the timer for another 2 minutes, continue to bake, and check again. Repeat this process until the cakes test done. The cake layers will probably take a total of 20 minutes. The timing may vary a minute or two depending on the cakes' positions in the oven. Using pot holders, carefully transfer the cakes to a wire rack.

PASTRY CHEF'S TIP

If the parchment paper used to line the pan sticks to the bottom of the cake, dip a pastry brush in warm water and lightly brush the paper. The water should loosen it, making it easier to remove without damaging the cake.

8 Unmold and cool the cakes

Let the cakes cool in the pans for 15 minutes. Run a thin knife along the inside edge of each pan to loosen the cake, keeping the knife pressed against the side. Invert a wire rack on top of 1 cake and invert together. The cake will release from the pan. Lift off the pan and peel off and discard the parchment. Using both hands, turn the cake layer top side up. Repeat with the second layer. Let cool completely on the racks, about 45 minutes. The cake layers will shrink slightly as they cool. The cakes are now ready to be filled and frosted.

9 Use or store the cakes

Fill and frost the cooled cake layers as directed in recipes. If not using the cake layers right away, store as directed on the opposite page.

Cooling & storing foam cakes

After the baked cake has cooled to the touch, you need to unmold it from the pan so that it can cool completely. It is important to cool cakes on racks, rather than directly on a work surface. The elevated wire-mesh construction allows air to circulate on all sides, promoting fast, even cooling and preventing sogginess. When it reaches room temperature, the cake is ready to be used or stored.

Releasing the cake from the pan (top left)
Run a thin knife along the inside edge of the pan to loosen the cake, keeping the knife pressed against the pan side. Invert a wire rack on top of the cake, then invert together. The cake will release from the pan. Lift off the pan.

Removing parchment paper (left)
Slowly and carefully peel off the parchment (baking) paper to speed cooling on the underside of the cake. Turn the cake top side up to cool.

Wrapping the cake for storage (above)
Tightly wrap the cooled cake layers individually in plastic wrap and store them at room temperature for up to 2 days.

Sponge Sheet Cake

Sponge cakes, perfect for cake layers, are also the choice for rolled cakes. Here an all-purpose vanilla or chocolate sponge cake is baked as a thin layer in a large, shallow baking pan. The batter bakes up light and tender but sturdy, making the finished sheet cake easy to roll with your choice of fillings and frostings.

1 Preheat the oven and prepare the pan
Position a rack in the middle of the oven, so the cake will be evenly surrounded with heat, and preheat to 350°F (180°C). Place a small amount of butter on a piece of waxed paper and spread the butter evenly over the bottom and sides of a 10-by-15-by-1-inch (25-by-38-by-2.5-cm) rimmed baking sheet. Line the bottom with parchment (baking) paper, butter the paper, then sprinkle it lightly with flour. Tap out the excess flour. For more details on preparing cake pans, turn to page 34.

2 Sift the dry ingredients
Suspend a fine-mesh sieve over a small bowl. If making chocolate sponge cake, add the flour, 2 tablespoons cocoa powder, the instant coffee powder, and salt. If making vanilla sponge cake, add the flour and salt. Lightly tap the rim of the sieve to encourage the ingredients to pass into the bowl. This both combines the ingredients and aerates the flour (compacted flour produces a less tender texture, or *crumb*). Set aside.

3 Beat the egg yolks with half the sugar
In a large mixing bowl or the bowl of a stand mixer, combine the 5 egg yolks and ⅓ cup (2½ oz/75 g) of the sugar. Fit the handheld mixer with the twin beaters or a stand mixer with the paddle attachment. Beat on medium-high speed until the batter is thickened and pale yellow and falls back on itself like a ribbon when the beaters are lifted, about 3 minutes. For more details on beating eggs to the ribbon stage, turn to page 37. Stop the mixer occasionally and, using a rubber spatula, scrape down the bowl sides. Add the vanilla extract and beat until combined. If using the stand mixer, use a spatula to scrape the yolk mixture into a large bowl. Wash the mixer bowl well to ensure that it is spotlessly clean and dry thoroughly. ›

Unsalted butter and flour for preparing the pan

For chocolate sponge sheet cake

½ cup (2 oz/60 g) cake (soft-wheat) flour

2 tablespoons Dutch-process cocoa powder, plus 1 tablespoon if storing the cake

¼ teaspoon instant coffee powder

Pinch of salt

4 large eggs, separated (page 36), plus 1 large egg yolk, at room temperature

⅔ cup (5 oz/155 g) granulated sugar

½ teaspoon vanilla extract (essence)

For vanilla sponge sheet cake

⅔ cup (2½ oz/75 g) cake (soft-wheat) flour

Pinch of salt

4 large eggs, separated (page 36), plus 1 large egg yolk, at room temperature

⅔ cup (5 oz/155 g) granulated sugar

½ teaspoon vanilla extract (essence)

1 tablespoon confectioners' (icing) sugar if storing the cake

MAKES ONE 10-BY-15-INCH (25-BY-38-CM) SHEET CAKE

RECOMMENDED USES
Bûche de Noël (page 113), Chocolate-Berry Cake Roll and other variations, (pages 118–119).

When folding, always add the lighter of the two mixtures on top and use a gentle folding motion. Otherwise, the batter will deflate.

For the best results, fold quickly and always stop folding as soon as the mixtures are just blended. You will be able to tell when no lighter streaks remain in the darker mixture.

4 Beat the egg whites with the remaining sugar

To the clean stand mixer bowl or a large mixing bowl, add the egg whites. Fit the mixer with the whip attachment. Beat on medium speed until foamy, about 1 minute. Increase the speed to medium-high and continue beating, moving the whip around the bowl if necessary, until the whites look shiny and smooth and hold slightly bent peaks—*soft peaks*—when you stop the mixer and lift the whip, 2–3 minutes. Turn the mixer on medium speed and beat in the remaining ½ cup sugar at a rate of about 2 tablespoons every 15 seconds. After all of the sugar has been incorporated, beat the whites for 1 minute longer. When you stop the mixer and lift the whip, the peaks will be firm and straight; these are *stiff peaks*. For more details on whipping egg whites, turn to page 37.

5 Fold the egg whites into the egg yolks

Using a rubber spatula, pile about one-third of the egg whites on top of the yolk mixture. Then, using the spatula, fold the mixtures together: Slice down through the center to the bottom of the bowl, pull the spatula to the side, and, keeping the flat side of the spatula against the side of the bowl, bring the spatula up and over the top of the egg whites, bringing some of the yolk mixture with it. Rotate the bowl a quarter turn and repeat the folding action until no white streaks remain. This first addition will lighten the batter. Now, pile the remaining egg whites on top of the mixture and fold them in using the same technique. If you need help with the folding technique, turn to page 39.

6 Fold in the flour mixture

Still using the spatula, fold in the cocoa mixture or flour mixture in 4 additions: Sprinkle about one-fourth of the mixture over the egg mixture, then, using the same technique as above, fold in the flour mixture just until no streaks of cocoa powder or flour are visible. Repeat with the remaining cocoa or flour mixture. Adding the dry ingredients in small amounts prevents their weight from deflating the egg mixture. The batter will be light and foamy.

PASTRY CHEF'S TIP
To bring cold eggs up to room temperature quickly, put whole eggs in a bowl of lukewarm water (hot water might cook them) for 30 minutes.

7 Bake the cake

Pour the batter into the prepared pan. Use the spatula to scrape every last bit from the bowl and then to smooth the surface lightly (it does not need to be perfectly smooth). Bake the cake undisturbed for 12 minutes. If the cake looks set and the surface is lightly browned, touch the top gently. If it feels firm, insert a thin skewer or toothpick in the center. If it comes out dry, the cake is done. If it comes out wet or with crumbs clinging to it, set the timer for another 2 minutes, continue to bake, and check again. Repeat this process until the cake tests done. The cake will probably take a total of 14 minutes.

8 Cool and unmold the cake

Using pot holders, carefully transfer the sheet cake to a wire rack. Let the cake cool in the pan until cool to the touch, about 25 minutes. The cake will shrink slightly as it cools. Run a thin knife along the inside edge of the pan to loosen the cake, keeping the knife pressed against the side. Invert a wire rack on top of the cake and invert together. Lift off the pan and peel off and discard the parchment. Using both hands, carefully turn the cake top side up. The cake is now ready to be filled and rolled.

9 Use or store the cake

Fill and frost the cooled sheet cake as directed in the recipe. If not using right away, store as directed on the opposite page.

PASTRY CHEF'S TIP

To prevent a sheet cake from sticking to the sides of the pan, run your finger around the edge of the pan immediately after the batter has been poured. This will help prevent the batter from adhering to the sides of the pan during baking.

Rolling & storing sheet cakes

Sheet cakes are usually formed into rolled cakes, such as Bûche de Noël, (page 113). To prevent cracking, they should be rolled while still warm and easy to shape. If any cracks form, they can be covered up when the cake is frosted. Waxed paper, along with cocoa powder for chocolate cakes, or confectioners' sugar for vanilla cakes, will keep the cake from sticking when it is rolled.

Dusting the top of the cake (top left)
Pour 1 tablespoon cocoa powder, for a chocolate cake, or confectioners' (icing) sugar, for a vanilla cake, into a fine-mesh sieve and tap lightly to dust the top of the cake.

Rolling the cake in waxed paper (left)
Cut two 21-inch (53-cm) sheets of waxed paper. Lightly dust 1 sheet with cocoa powder or confectioners' sugar. Carefully place the cake, top side up, on the dusted paper. Top with the second sheet. Starting from a long side, roll up the cake.

Sealing the cake in waxed paper (above)
Fold the ends of the paper under the cake. Store at room temperature for up to 2 days.

Génoise

Génoise is a type of sponge cake that relies on the steady, vigorous beating of whole eggs and sugar to reach its light and elegant loft. The addition of melted butter ensures a tender crumb. Consider génoise a "palette" that takes well to mixing and matching with different syrups, fillings, and frostings.

1 **Preheat the oven and prepare the pans**
Position a rack in the middle of the oven, so the cake layers will be evenly surrounded with heat, and preheat to 350°F (180°C). Place a small amount of butter on a piece of waxed paper and spread the butter evenly over the bottom and sides of two 9-inch (23-cm) round layer cake pans. Line the bottoms with parchment (baking) paper, butter the paper, then sprinkle lightly with flour. Tap out the excess flour. For more details on preparing cake pans, turn to page 34.

2 **Melt the butter and sift the dry ingredients**
Put the butter pieces in a small saucepan, place over low heat, and heat until the butter melts. Remove from the heat and set aside. Suspend a fine-mesh sieve over a small bowl and add the flour. Lightly tap the rim of the sieve to encourage the flour to pass into the bowl, which both combines ingredients and aerates the flour (compacted flour produces a less tender texture, or *crumb*). Set aside.

3 **Set up a double boiler**
Select a saucepan and a deep stainless-steel bowl (or the bowl of a stand mixer) that fits snugly in the rim of the pan. (A heatproof glass bowl can be used, too, although the metal bowl will conduct heat faster.) The bottom of the bowl should reach about halfway down in the saucepan. Remove the bowl, fill the saucepan about one-third full with water—the water must not touch the bottom of the bowl when the bowl is added—and heat the water over low heat just until you see small bubbles break the surface of the water; this is a *simmer*.

4 **Warm the eggs and sugar**
Meanwhile, put the bowl on a work surface and break the eggs into it. Using a balloon whisk, mix until the yolks and whites are well blended. Pour in the sugar and whisk to combine. Place over the simmering water. Whisking constantly, yet slowly and gently, heat the egg mixture until it feels comfortably warm and the sugar is dissolved, about 3 minutes. To test, dip a finger into the eggs to check their warmth (for accuracy, you can insert an instant-read thermometer into the mixture; it should register about 120°F/49°C). Warming the yolk mixture stabilizes it and makes it easier to aerate it and increase in volume. ›

Unsalted butter and flour for preparing the pans

4 tablespoons (2 oz/60 g) unsalted butter, cut into 4 equal pieces

1½ cups (6 oz/185 g) cake (soft-wheat) flour

8 large eggs

1⅓ cups (11 oz/345 g) granulated sugar

1 teaspoon vanilla extract (essence)

MAKES TWO 9-INCH (23-CM) ROUND LAYERS

PASTRY CHEF'S TIP
Like sponge cake, génoise can also be made as a chocolate version. When readying your mise en place, *make the following alterations: First, reduce the cake (soft-wheat) flour to 1 cup (4 oz/125 g). Next, add ½ cup (1½ oz/45 g) Dutch-process cocoa powder. Finally, reduce the sugar to 1½ cups (12 oz/375 g). Proceed with the recipe, adding the cocoa powder with the flour.*

RECOMMENDED USES
Lemon Meringue Cake (page 110), and Double Chocolate Layer Cake (page 110).

Aerate the egg mixture

5 Using pot holders, remove the bowl from over the water. Fit a handheld mixer with the twin beaters or a stand mixer with the paddle attachment. (If using the stand mixer, transfer the warm egg mixture to the stand mixer bowl.) Beat the egg mixture on medium-high speed until it is thickened, pale yellow, and the batter falls back on itself like a ribbon when the beaters are lifted, about 5 minutes. If you are not sure it is sufficiently thickened, continue beating for another minute or two; it is difficult to overbeat the mixture. For more details on beating eggs to the ribbon stage, turn to page 37.

Fold in the dry ingredients

6 Holding a fine-mesh sieve over the whipped eggs, add about one-third of the sifted flour to the sieve. Lightly tap the rim of the sieve so the flour falls onto the eggs. Then, using a rubber spatula, gently fold the mixtures together: Slice down through the center to the bottom of the bowl, pull the spatula to the side, and, keeping the flat side of the spatula against side of the bowl, bring the spatula up and over the top of the flour, bringing some of the egg mixture with it. Rotate the bowl a quarter turn and repeat the folding action until no white streaks of flour remain. Repeat the folding process with the remaining flour in 2 equal additions. Be sure every bit of the flour is fully incorporated, or it can form lumps when the butter is added in the next step. If you need help with the folding technique, turn to page 39.

Fold in the wet ingredients

7 If the butter has hardened during sitting, reheat it over low heat just until it is liquid. Drizzle the melted butter and vanilla extract over the center of the batter. Using the rubber spatula and the same folding motion as for the flour, fold the butter and vanilla into the batter until they are no longer visible.

PASTRY CHEF'S TIP
If you are unable to find cake flour, you can substitute all-purpose (plain) flour. It is heavier, however, so you need to adjust the amount. Use ¾ cup (3 oz/90 g) sifted all-purpose flour plus 2 tablespoons cornstarch (cornflour) for every 1 cup (4 oz/125 g) cake flour.

8 Bake the cake layers

Pour the batter into the prepared pans, dividing it evenly. Use the spatula to scrape every last bit from the bowl and then to smooth the surface lightly (it does not need to be perfectly smooth.) Bake the cakes undisturbed for 18 minutes. If the layers look lightly browned and set—that is, the batter no longer looks liquid—touch the tops gently. If they feel firm, insert a thin skewer or toothpick into the centers. If it comes out dry, the cakes are done. If it comes out wet or with crumbs clinging to it, set the timer for another 2 minutes, continue to bake, and check again. Repeat this process until the cakes test done, probably a total of 20 minutes. The timing may vary a minute or two depending on the position in the oven. Because of the large number of eggs in a génoise batter, the finished cake should rise to twice the height of the prebaked batter. Using pot holders, carefully transfer the cakes to a wire rack.

PASTRY CHEF'S TIP

Resist the urge to open the oven door during the first 15 minutes of baking any cake. Changes in air pressure or temperature can prevent the cake from rising properly.

9 Unmold and cool the cakes

Let the cakes cool in the pans for 10 minutes. Run a thin knife along the inside edge of each pan to loosen the cake, keeping the knife pressed against the pan side. Invert a wire rack on top of 1 cake and invert together. The cake will release from the pan. Lift off the pan and peel off and discard the parchment. Using both hands, carefully turn the cake layer top side up. Repeat with the second layer. Let cool completely on the racks, about 45 minutes. The cakes are now ready to be filled and frosted.

10 Use or store the cake layers

Fill and frost the cooled cake layers as directed in recipes. Or, you can store them before using (see the opposite page).

Working with génoise

Génoise is a sturdy cake that gains a lot of height from the large number of eggs that go into the batter. This makes it an excellent cake to cut into layers. Typically, génoise is a dry cake, which means it should be brushed with a flavored syrup. Traditional French bakers cut off the top of the cake to give it a more finished look. You can follow their example, especially if it is uneven or has ragged edges, or you can leave it intact.

Cutting the cake top (top left)
If the top of the cake has ragged edges or is uneven, use a serrated knife to cut a thin, even layer around the circumference.

Stacking the cake layers for storage (left)
To economize on storage space, stack the cake layers on top of one another, separating each layer with a piece of waxed paper. Wrap the layers tightly in plastic wrap and store at room temperature for up to 2 days.

Brushing the layers with cake syrup (above)
Before using the layers, use a clean pastry brush, free of any odors, to brush a flavorful syrup on top of the cake.

Classic Butter Cake

A generous measure of butter in this cake gives it a particularly fine-grained, moist texture. Unlike a génoise or a sponge cake, both of which rely on beaten eggs for their loft, this sunny yellow cake uses a chemical leavener, baking powder, for the height. Choose the formula for either one cake or two, depending on your needs.

1 Preheat the oven and prepare the pan(s)
Position a rack in the middle of the oven and preheat to 350°F (180°C). Butter one or two 9-inch (23-cm) round layer cake pan(s). Line the pan(s) with parchment (baking) paper. Butter the paper, sprinkle lightly with flour, and then tap out the extra flour. For more details on preparing pans, turn to page 34.

2 Sift the dry ingredients
Suspend a fine-mesh sieve over a small bowl and add the flour, baking powder, and salt. Lightly tap the rim of the sieve to encourage the ingredients to pass into the bowl. Set aside.

3 Make the batter
In the bowl of a stand mixer or a large mixing bowl, combine the butter and sugar. Fit the stand mixer with the paddle attachment or a handheld mixer with the twin beaters. Beat on medium speed until the mixture is light and airy and changes from light yellow to cream, about 2 minutes. If using a handheld mixer, move the beaters around in the bowl to evenly beat the mixture. (For more details on creaming butter, turn to page 38.) Add the eggs one at a time, beating for 1 minute after each addition. Stop the mixer occasionally to scrape any batter from the sides of the bowl. After all of the eggs have been added, add the vanilla extract and beat for another minute. Reduce the mixer speed to low. Add one-third of the dry ingredients and mix until incorporated. Next, add one-half of the milk and mix until incorporated. Continue alternately adding the ingredients in the same manner, ending with the last third of the dry ingredients.

4 Bake, unmold, and cool the cake(s)
Pour the batter evenly into the prepared pan(s) and smooth the top with a spatula. Bake undisturbed for 30 minutes. If each cake looks set and the top is lightly browned, insert a thin skewer or toothpick in the center. If it comes out dry, the cake is done. If it comes out wet or with crumbs clinging to it, continue to bake in 5 minute increments until it tests done. Using pot holders, transfer the cake(s) to a wire rack. Let cool for 15 minutes. Run a thin knife along the inside edge of the pan. Invert a wire rack on top of the cake(s) and invert together. Lift off the pan(s) and peel off the parchment. Turn the cake(s) top side up and let cool on the rack for about 45 minutes.

5 Use or store the cake(s)
Use the cake(s) as directed in recipes. Or, tightly wrap the cooled cake(s) in plastic wrap and store at room temperature for up to 2 days.

For 1 cake layer

Unsalted butter and flour for preparing the pan

1¼ cups (5 oz/155 g) plus 2 tablespoons cake (soft-wheat) flour

1 teaspoon baking powder

⅛ teaspoon salt

½ cup (4 oz/125 g) unsalted butter, at room temperature

1 cup (8 oz/250 g) granulated sugar

2 large eggs, at room temperature

1 teaspoon vanilla extract (essence)

½ cup (4 fl oz/125 ml) whole milk, at room temperature

For 2 cake layers

Unsalted butter and flour for preparing the pan(s)

2¾ cups (11 oz/345 g) cake (soft-wheat) flour

2 teaspoons baking powder

¼ teaspoon salt

1 cup (8 oz/250 g) unsalted butter, at room temperature

2 cups (1 lb/500 g) granulated sugar

4 large eggs, at room temperature

2 teaspoons vanilla extract (essence)

1 cup (8 fl oz/250 ml) whole milk, at room temperature

MAKES ONE OR TWO 9-INCH (23-CM) ROUND LAYER(S)

RECOMMENDED USES
Pineapple Upside-Down Cake (page 67), and Boston Cream Pie (page 128).

Devil's Food Cake

Rich and delicious, this cake is a favorite with almost anyone. It gets its distinctive reddish brown color from the interaction of the unsweetened chocolate and the alkaline baking soda in the batter. The addition of brown sugar both sweetens and deepens the cake's overall flavor, while the liberal use of butter and eggs guarantees a moist and tender texture and rich flavor.

Unsalted butter and flour for preparing the pans

2¼ cups (9 oz/280 g) cake (soft-wheat) flour

1 teaspoon baking soda (bicarbonate of soda)

¼ teaspoon salt

1 cup (8 oz/250 g) unsalted butter, at room temperature

1 cup (7 oz/220 g) firmly packed light brown sugar

¾ cup (6 oz/185 g) granulated sugar

4 large eggs, at room temperature

2 teaspoons vanilla extract (essence)

4 oz (125 g) unsweetened chocolate, chopped and melted (page 40)

1 cup (8 fl oz/250 ml) low-fat or nonfat buttermilk, at room temperature

MAKES TWO 9-INCH (23-CM) ROUND LAYERS

RECOMMENDED USES
Triple Chocolate Layer Cake, page 110. You could also make this cake using Chocolate Buttercream (page 22) to fill the layers and frost the cake.

1 **Preheat the oven and prepare the pans**
Position a rack in the middle of the oven and preheat to 350°F (180°C). Butter two 9-inch (23-cm) round layer cake pans. Line the pans with parchment (baking) paper. Butter the paper, sprinkle lightly with flour, and then tap out the extra flour. For more details on preparing pans, turn to page 34.

2 **Sift the dry ingredients**
Suspend a fine-mesh sieve over a small bowl and add the flour, baking soda, and salt. Lightly tap the rim of the sieve to encourage the ingredients to pass into the bowl. Set aside.

3 **Make the batter**
In the bowl of a stand mixer or a large mixing bowl, combine the butter and both sugars. Fit the stand mixer with the paddle attachment or a handheld mixer with the twin beaters. Beat on medium speed until the mixture is light and airy and lightens in color, about 2 minutes. If using a handheld mixer, move the beaters around in the bowl. (For more details on creaming butter, turn to page 38.) Add the eggs one at a time, beating for 1 minute after each addition. Stop the mixer occasionally to scrape the sides of the bowl. After all of the eggs have been added, add the vanilla extract and beat for 1 minute longer. Add the melted chocolate and mix on medium speed until the mixture is a uniform color. Reduce the mixer speed to low. Add the dry ingredients in 3 batches alternately with the buttermilk in 2 batches, beginning and ending with the dry ingredients and mixing each addition until incorporated before adding the next.

4 **Bake, unmold, and cool the cakes**
Pour the batter into the prepared pans and smooth the tops with a spatula. Bake for 30 minutes. If the cakes look set, insert a thin skewer or toothpick in the center. If it comes out dry, the cakes are done. If it comes out wet or with crumbs clinging to it, continue to bake until they test done. Using pot holders, transfer the cakes to a wire rack. Let cool for 15 minutes. Run a thin knife along the inside edge of the pans. One at a time, invert a wire rack on top of the cakes and invert together. Lift off the pans and peel off the parchment. Turn the cakes top side up and let cool on the rack for about 45 minutes.

5 **Use or store the cakes**
Use the cakes as directed in recipes. Or, tightly wrap the cooled cakes in plastic wrap and store at room temperature for up to 2 days.

5

Special Occasion Cakes

Now that you can bake round cakes and sheet cakes, you are ready to stack them or roll them with fillings and frostings, turning them into a four-layer Classic Birthday Cake or a Christmastime Bûche de Noël. Here, you'll also learn how to make Vanilla Cheesecake with a luscious sour cream topping, and decadent Individual Molten Chocolate Cakes—every recipe fit for a special occasion.

Classic Birthday Cake

This four-layer cake, which boasts a chocolate buttercream filling and a dark chocolate frosting, is my ideal birthday cake. For a kid-friendly version of the cake, omit the rum and coffee in the syrup and the coffee in the frosting and use the vanilla extract instead.

1 Make the cake syrup
In a small saucepan over low heat, combine the water and sugar. Heat, stirring often, until the sugar dissolves and the mixture is hot. Remove from the heat and stir in the coffee and rum or the vanilla extract. Let the syrup cool to room temperature, about 15 minutes.

2 Make the sugar syrup for the buttercream
In the bowl of a stand mixer or a large mixing bowl, use a whisk to blend the egg whites and cream of tartar until the cream of tartar dissolves, about 1 minute. Set the bowl aside. In a small, heavy-bottomed saucepan, combine the ⅔ cup sugar, the water, and the corn syrup. Cover the pan, place over low heat, and heat until the sugar dissolves, about 5 minutes. Uncover occasionally and stir with a wooden spoon. Raise the heat to high and let the syrup bubble vigorously, without stirring, until it is smooth and thick and registers 240°F (116°C) on a candy thermometer, about 5 minutes. Use a damp pastry brush to brush down any sugar crystals that form on the sides of the pan. Remove from the heat.

3 Combine the egg whites and sugar syrup
Fit a stand mixer or handheld mixer with the whip attachment. Beat the egg white mixture with the 2 tablespoons sugar on medium speed until foamy, about 1 minute. Increase the speed to medium-high and continue beating the egg whites until they look white, shiny, and smooth and soft peaks form when the whip is lifted, 2–3 minutes. Reduce the mixer speed to low and carefully pour the hot syrup in a thin stream in the space between the whip and the sides of the bowl; the bowl will feel hot to the touch. When all of the syrup has been added, increase the mixer speed to medium-low and beat for 5 minutes. At this point, the outside of the bowl will be lukewarm to the touch and the mixture will form stiff peaks when the whip is lifted.

4 Incorporate the butter for the buttercream
With the mixer on medium-high speed, add the butter to the egg white mixture 1 piece at a time. Beat until each piece is incorporated before adding the next piece. Stop the mixer occasionally and use a rubber spatula to scrape down the sides of the bowl. Add the coffee powder (if using), vanilla extract, and the melted chocolate and beat until combined. (If using a handheld mixer, move the beaters around in the bowl to ensure that every bit of the mixture is well beaten.) The buttercream should be soft enough to spread, but not pourable. If it is too soft, refrigerate for about 20 minutes to firm it slightly, then, just before using, whisk briefly until smooth. For more details on making buttercream, turn to page 22. ›

Vanilla Sponge Cake Layers (page 81), baked and cooled

For the syrup
½ cup (4 fl oz/125 ml) water

½ cup (4 oz/125 g) granulated sugar

2 tablespoons dark rum and 1 tablespoon instant coffee powder, or ½ teaspoon vanilla extract (essence)

For the chocolate buttercream
3 large egg whites (page 36)

¼ teaspoon cream of tartar

⅔ cup (5 oz/155 g) plus 2 tablespoons granulated sugar

¼ cup (2 fl oz/60 fl oz) water

1 tablespoon light corn syrup

1¼ cups (10 oz/315 g) unsalted butter, at room temperature, cut into 10 equal pieces

1 teaspoon vanilla extract (essence)

8 oz (250 g) semisweet (plain) chocolate or white chocolate, chopped and melted (page 40)

For the chocolate frosting
2 cups (8 oz/250 g) confectioners' (icing) sugar, sifted

1 cup (8 oz/250 g) unsalted butter, at room temperature

2 teaspoons vanilla extract (essence)

1 teaspoon instant coffee powder, optional

4 oz (125 g) unsweetened chocolate, chopped and melted (page 40)

¼ cup (2 fl oz/60 ml) heavy (double) cream, at room temperature

MAKES ONE 9-INCH (23-CM) CAKE, OR 12 SERVINGS

5 Make the chocolate frosting

In the bowl of a stand mixer or a large mixing bowl, combine the confectioners' sugar and butter. Fit the stand mixer with the paddle attachment or the handheld mixer with the twin beaters. Beat on low speed until combined, then continue beating until smooth, about 1 minute. Add the vanilla extract and instant coffee, if using, and beat on low speed until well mixed. Add the melted chocolate and beat until fully incorporated and the color is uniform. Pour in the cream, increase the mixer speed to medium, and beat until the color lightens and the mixture looks fluffy, about 1 minute. Use the frosting as soon as possible, while it is still soft and spreads easily.

6 Cut each cake into 2 layers

If you need help splitting a cake into layers, turn to page 42. Place 1 cooled cake on a flat work surface. Hold a ruler alongside it to measure its height and, using toothpicks, mark the midpoint at 4–6 equally spaced intervals around the cake. The picks will guide you as you cut the single cake into 2 uniform layers. Using a large serrated knife and a sawing motion, cut the layer in half horizontally to make 2 layers. Place a large sheet of waxed paper on the work surface, lift off the top cake, and place cut side up on the waxed paper. Place the bottom layer, cut side up, alongside it. Split the remaining cake in the same way and add the layers to the waxed paper, keeping one cut side down (this will be the top of the cake).

7 Prepare to build the cake

Using a clean pastry brush, brush the top of each of the 4 layers lightly with the cake syrup, using about 3 tablespoons syrup for each layer. The syrup will moisten and add flavor to the cake. Place 4 strips of waxed paper, each cut 2 inches (5 cm) wide, about 1 inch (2.5 cm) on a cake stand or plate. Slide a cake layer, syrup side up, onto the waxed paper strips. The layers are sturdy, but if you are concerned about them cracking, use 2 wide metal spatulas or the removable bottom of a tart pan to help in the transfer.

PASTRY CHEF'S TIP

If you don't own a cake stand, you can improvise by turning the cake pan in which the cake was baked upside down and placing the cake on top of it, to give it added height.

8 Fill and frost the cakes

Spoon 1 cup (8 fl oz/250 ml) of the chocolate buttercream into a small bowl and set aside. Using an offset spatula, mound about 1¼ cups (10 fl oz/310 ml) of the buttercream in the center of the cake and evenly spread it to the edges. Position a second cake layer on top of the buttercream, lining up the edges. Spread another 1¼ cups buttercream over it in the same manner. Repeat with the bottom half of the remaining cake layer and the remaining buttercream. Position the final layer on top. Using a clean spatula and about 1 cup of the frosting, spread the top and sides of the cake with a thin layer of frosting to seal in the crumbs (this is called a *crumb coat*). Spoon about half of the remaining frosting in the center of the cake and, using broad strokes, spread it over the top. Holding the spatula nearly perpendicular to the top, spread the remaining frosting over the sides of the cake, turning the plate as needed to frost the sides evenly. For more details on filling and frosting a cake, turn to page 43.

PASTRY CHEF'S TIP

If you are new to piping, practice on a piece of waxed paper before you decorate a frosted cake. You can also experiment with different tips. When you have finished practicing, scrape the frosting back into the pastry bag so none is wasted.

9 Finish and decorate the cake

Smooth over the top and sides one last time to provide a smooth finish for the decoration. If you are not sure how to fill and pipe with a pastry (piping) bag, turn to pages 44–45. Fit a pastry bag with a small fluted tip, secure it with the coupler, if needed, and fold down the top. Scoop the reserved buttercream into the pastry bag, unfold the bag, and twist the top, pressing the buttercream toward the tip. Pipe a shell border on the top and bottom edge of the cake (see opposite page), or choose a different decorative design from the ideas on page 45.

10 Serve the cake

Carefully pull out the waxed paper strips from under the cake and discard. Using a large, sharp knife and a light sawing motion, cut the cake into 12 wedges. Or, carefully place on a cake plate with a lid and refrigerate for up to 3 days; bring to room temperature before serving to soften the buttercream and frosting.

Serving ideas

I believe that simple decorations are best, so that the flavor and texture of a layer cake can star. You can decorate each slice with colorful garnishes such as an assortment of sugared flowers. A sprinkle of dark chocolate curls on top of the cake or on individual slices also makes an attractive— and delicious—presentation. A pretty piped shell border adds celebratory flair and, with a little practice, is easy to do.

Cake slices with sugared flowers (top left)
Top each slice with a few sugared flowers (page 30). Pale-colored flowers provide an appealing contrast.

Cake slices with chocolate curls (left)
Make dark or white chocolate curls (page 45) and refrigerate for a few minutes to harden them. Sprinkle the curls lightly on each slice.

Cake slices with a shell border (above)
Pipe a mound of frosting about ½ inch (12 mm) long, then pull the bag up and toward you, lessening the pressure and lowering the angle of the pastry bag slightly to form a tail on the shell. Repeat to form 2 borders of shells, one each around the top and bottom of the cake.

Layer Cake Variations

You now have learned several important skills—baking and splitting cake layers; making buttercream, ganache, and citrus curd; and frosting and decorating cakes—that can be combined to make a wide range of layer cakes. The six variations that follow show how easy it is to mix and match a variety of components. For example, Double Chocolate Layer Cake calls for génoise layers, white chocolate buttercream, and a swirl of chocolate curls; Coconut Layer Cake spreads sponge cake layers with lime curd and finishes the cake with coconut buttercream and shredded coconut; and Black Forest Cake fills the layers with fresh cherries and cream. Each variation makes 12 servings.

Double Chocolate Layer Cake

The outside of this cake appears deceptively pale. When cut, it reveals more traditional chocolate layers.

Bake and cool 2 Génoise cake layers, chocolate version (page 93).

Next, make a chocolate syrup: In a small saucepan, stir together ¼ cup (2 fl oz/ 60 ml) water and ¼ cup (2 oz/ 60 g) granulated sugar over low heat until the sugar dissolves and the mixture is hot. Stir in 2 tablespoons crème de cacao and let cool.

Make 1 batch Chocolate Buttercream (page 22), replacing the dark chocolate with 8 oz (250 g) melted white chocolate.

When ready to assemble, brush about 3 tablespoons chocolate syrup onto the top of each cake layer (you don't need to split them).

Finally, spread about 1½ cups (12 fl oz/ 375 ml) of the buttercream over 1 cake. Place the second layer on top. Frost the cake with the remaining buttercream. Spoon 2 cups (4 oz/125 g) white chocolate curls (page 45) on top of the cake, then cut into slices and serve.

Triple Chocolate Layer Cake

Chocolate cake layers, chocolate ganache, and chocolate frosting make this the quintessential chocolate cake.

Bake and cool 2 Devil's Food Cake layers (page 100).

Next, make a coffee syrup: In a small saucepan, stir together ¼ cup (2 fl oz/ 60 ml) water and ¼ cup (2 oz/ 60 g) granulated sugar over low heat until the sugar dissolves and the mixture is hot. Stir in ½ tablespoon instant coffee powder and let cool.

Make 1 batch Ganache (page 28), then chill and whip it. Follow step 5 to make Chocolate Frosting.

When ready to assemble, brush about 3 tablespoons coffee syrup onto the top of each cake layer (you don't need to split them).

Finally, spread the ganache over 1 cake layer. Place the second layer on top. Use the frosting to frost the cake, then cut into slices and serve.

Lemon Meringue Cake

If Meyer lemons are available, use them for the cake syrup and lemon curd.

Bake and cool 2 Génoise cake layers (page 93).

Next, make a lemon syrup: In a small saucepan, stir together ½ cup (4 fl oz/ 125 ml) water and ½ cup (4 oz/ 125 g) granulated sugar over low heat until the sugar dissolves and the mixture is hot. Stir in 3 tablespoons fresh lemon juice and let cool.

Make 1 batch Citrus Curd (page 26) using lemons and refrigerate to chill.

When ready to assemble, cut the cakes into 2 layers each, to make 4 layers. Brush about 3 tablespoons lemon syrup onto the top of each layer. Spread one-third of the lemon curd over 1 cake layer. Top with a second layer and spread with another one-third of the curd. Top with a third cake layer and spread with the remaining curd. Top with the fourth layer.

Finally, make 1 batch Meringue Frosting (page 24) and use it to frost the cake. Gently dip a small spoon into the top of the cake to make attractive swirls. Cut into slices and serve.

Coconut Layer Cake

Layers of coconut buttercream and lime curd fill this cake, then it's coated with shredded coconut for extra flavor and a shaggy look.

Bake and cool 2 Vanilla Sponge Cake Layers (page 81).

Next, make a lime syrup: In a small saucepan, stir together ½ cup (4 fl oz/ 125 ml) water and ½ cup (4 oz/ 125 g) granulated sugar over low heat until the sugar dissolves and the mixture is hot. Stir in 3 tablespoons fresh lime juice and let cool.

Make 1 batch Citrus Curd (page 26) using limes, and put it in the refrigerator to chill. Make 1 batch Vanilla Buttercream (page 20) and stir in 1 teaspoon coconut extract (essence) until blended.

When ready to assemble, cut the cakes into 2 layers each, to make 4 layers. Brush about 3 tablespoons lime syrup onto the top of each layer. Spread one-third of the lime curd over 1 cake layer. Top with a second layer and spread with another one-third of the curd. Top with a third cake layer and spread with the remaining curd. Top with the fourth layer.

Finally, frost the cake with the coconut buttercream. Using the palm of your hand, gently press 2 cups (8 oz/250 g) sweetened shredded dried coconut onto the sides and top of the cake. Cut into slices and serve.

Banana Layer Cake

You get a triple dose of banana with this cake: banana cake syrup, banana buttercream, and fresh banana slices sandwiched between the layers.

Bake and cool 2 Vanilla Sponge Cake Layers (page 81).

Next, make a banana syrup: In a small saucepan, stir together ¼ cup (2 fl oz/ 60 ml) water and ¼ cup (2 oz/ 60 g) granulated sugar over low heat until the sugar dissolves and the mixture is hot. Stir in 2 tablespoons banana liqueur and let cool.

Make 1 batch Vanilla Buttercream (page 20), but use only 1 teaspoon vanilla extract (essence) and stir in 2 tablespoons banana liqueur until blended.

When ready to assemble, brush about 3 tablespoons banana syrup onto the top of each cake layer (you don't need to split them).

Spread about 1½ cups (12 fl oz/375 ml) of the banana buttercream over 1 cake layer. Arrange 2 peeled and sliced bananas (½-inch/12-mm slices) in an even layer over the buttercream and press them gently into the buttercream to level the filling. Top with the second cake layer.

Finally, frost the cake with the remaining banana buttercream. Cut into slices and serve.

> **PASTRY CHEF'S TIP**
> *To give your frosted cake a high-gloss finish, use a blow dryer set on medium heat over the entire outside of the frosted cake until it has a glossy appearance. Serve immediately.*

Black Forest Cake

This cake combines two complementary flavors: chocolate and cherry.

Bake and cool 2 Chocolate Sponge Cake Layers (page 81).

Next, make a cherry syrup: In a small saucepan, stir together ¼ cup (2 fl oz/ 60 ml) water and ¼ cup (2 oz/ 60 g) granulated sugar over low heat until the sugar dissolves and the mixture is hot. Stir in 2 tablespoons kirsch.

Pit and halve ½ lb (250 g) Bing cherries and add to the syrup. Let stand for about 30 minutes. Suspend a fine-mesh sieve over a small bowl and pour the cherry mixture through it. Set the cherries aside and let the syrup cool.

Combine 2½ cups (20 fl oz/625 ml) heavy (double) cream, 3 tablespoons confectioners' (icing) sugar, and 1 tablespoon kirsch in a stainless-steel or glass bowl. Using a mixer fitted with the whip attachment on medium-high speed or a balloon whisk, beat the mixture until it forms soft peaks.

When ready to assemble, brush about 3 tablespoons cherry syrup onto the top of each cake layer (you don't need to split them).

Spread about 1½ cups (12 fl oz/375 ml) of the whipped cream evenly over 1 cake layer. Arrange the cherry halves in an even layer over the whipped cream and press them gently into the cream to level the filling. Top with the second cake layer.

Finally, frost the cake with the remaining whipped cream. Cut into slices and serve.

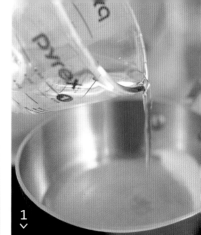

Bûche de Noël

A light sponge sheet cake forms the base for this traditional French Christmas dessert that is shaped and decorated to recall an old-fashioned holiday yule log. The frosting and garnish of thick and creamy buttercream and delicate chocolate curls deliver both richness and texture.

1 Make the cake syrup

While the cake is cooling, make the syrup: In a small saucepan over low heat, combine the water and sugar. Heat, stirring often, until the sugar dissolves and the mixture is hot, about 2–3 minutes. Remove from the heat and stir in the rum. Let the syrup cool to room temperature, about 15 minutes.

2 Make the sugar syrup for the buttercream

In the bowl of a stand mixer or a large mixing bowl, use a whisk to blend the egg whites and cream of tartar until the cream of tartar dissolves, about 1 minute. Set the bowl aside. In a small, heavy-bottomed saucepan, combine the ⅔ cup sugar, the water, and the corn syrup. Cover the pan, place over low heat, and heat until the sugar is dissolved, about 5 minutes. Uncover occasionally and stir with a wooden spoon. Raise the heat to high and let the syrup bubble vigorously, without stirring, until it is smooth and thick and reads 240°F (116°C) on a candy thermometer, about 5 minutes. Use a damp pastry brush to brush down any sugar crystals that form on the sides of the pan. Remove from the heat.

3 Combine the egg whites and sugar syrup

Fit a stand mixer or handheld mixer with the whip attachment. Beat the egg white mixture with 2 tablespoons sugar on medium speed until foamy, about 1 minute. Increase the speed to medium-high and continue beating the egg whites until they look white, shiny, and smooth and soft peaks form when the whip is lifted, 2–3 minutes. Reduce the mixer speed to low and carefully pour the hot syrup in a thin stream in the space between the whip and the sides of the bowl; the bowl will feel hot to the touch. When all of the syrup has been added, increase the mixer speed to medium-low and beat for 5 minutes. At this point, the outside of the bowl will be lukewarm to the touch and the mixture will form stiff peaks when the whip is lifted.

4 Incorporate the butter and chocolate for the buttercream

With the mixer on medium-high speed, add the butter to the egg white mixture 1 piece at a time. Beat until each piece is incorporated before adding the next piece. Stop the mixer occasionally and use a rubber spatula to scrape down the sides of the bowl. Add the vanilla extract and the melted chocolate and beat until combined. (If using a handheld mixer, move the beaters around in the bowl to ensure that every bit of the mixture is well beaten.) The buttercream should be soft enough to spread, but not pourable. If it is too soft, refrigerate for about 20 minutes to firm it slightly, then, just before using, whisk briefly until smooth. For more details on making chocolate buttercream, turn to page 22.

One Vanilla Sponge Sheet Cake (page 87), baked and cooled

For the rum cake syrup

¼ cup (2 fl oz/60 ml) water

¼ cup (2 fl oz/60 g) granulated sugar

4 teaspoons dark rum

For the chocolate buttercream

3 cold large egg whites (page 36)

¼ teaspoon cream of tartar

⅔ cup (5 oz/155 g) plus 2 tablespoons granulated sugar

¼ cup (2 fl oz/60 fl oz) water

1 tablespoon light corn syrup

1¼ cups (10 oz/315 g) unsalted butter, at room temperature, cut into 10 equal pieces

1 teaspoon vanilla extract (essence)

8 oz (250 g) semisweet (plain) chocolate or white chocolate, chopped and melted (page 40)

For the chocolate curls

4 oz (125 g) block semisweet (plain) or bittersweet chocolate

MAKES ONE 12-INCH (30-CM) CAKE ROLL, OR 10–12 SERVINGS

5

6

5 Make the chocolate curls

Soften the chocolate slightly by holding it in your hands for a minute or two to warm it, or by putting it on a plate in a sunny window for 5–15 minutes. Its exterior should feel slightly sticky. Line a rimmed baking sheet with parchment (baking) paper. Holding the chocolate block with one hand, and using a vegetable peeler, scrape curls from the block of chocolate. Use strokes 1½–2 inches (4–5 cm) long, and move the peeler toward you, turning the block so that you scrape from all sides to form curls. As the curls are cut, let them fall on the work surface. Carefully transfer the curls to the parchment-lined baking sheet, keeping them in a single layer. Place the pan in the freezer for about 30 minutes to firm the curls. For more information on making chocolate curls, turn to page 45.

6 Fill the cake roll

Cut a piece of waxed paper about 6 inches (15 cm) longer than the rimmed baking sheet and place it horizontally on a work surface. Transfer the cake—it should still be slightly warm for easier rolling—to the waxed paper. Using a pastry brush, lightly brush the top with two-thirds of the cake syrup. (If you have baked the cake ahead of time (see page 91) unroll it and remove the top sheet of waxed paper.) Using a heatproof spatula, scoop 2 cups (16 fl oz/500 ml) of the buttercream onto the center. Then, using an offset or icing spatula, spread it evenly over the cake. Resist the urge to use more filling, as it will make rolling more difficult and may ooze out the ends.

7 Roll up the cake

Starting at the long side closest to you, roll up the cake onto itself, carefully moving your hands from one end of the roll to the other to create an even cylinder. You can lift the waxed paper to help get the roll started, but leave the paper behind as the roll takes shape. Do not worry if small cracks or tears form; the frosting will cover any imperfections.

8 Make the cake "knot"

Place the cake roll seam side down on a cutting board. Using a large, sharp knife, a light sawing motion, and cutting at a 20-degree angle, cut a slice about 1½ inches (4 cm) thick off one end of the cake roll. This will be used to simulate a knot on the yule log. Using the icing spatula, spread about 1 tablespoon of the buttercream on top of the roll, positioning it about 3 inches (7.5 cm) from one of the ends. Press the knot onto the buttercream to secure it in place.

PASTRY CHEF'S TIP
You can store leftover cake syrup in a tightly covered container in the refrigerator for up to 6 months. Use it for other cakes or to flavor drinks, such as coffee or club soda.

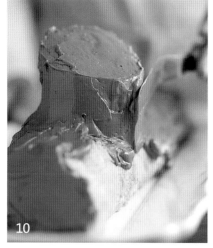

9 Brush the outside of the cake with syrup

Using the pastry brush, brush the outside of the cake roll evenly with the remaining cake syrup, taking care to avoid the buttercream. The syrup will further moisten and add flavor to the cake.

10 Frost the cake

Using a wide spatula, slide the cake roll onto a long platter. Using a small offset or icing spatula, spread the remaining buttercream over the entire cake, covering the knot and ends completely.

11 Garnish the cake

Using the spatula, make a series of swirls in the buttercream on top of the knot and at each end of the cake to resemble tree rings. Then, run the tines of a fork down the length of the cake all over its surface to simulate the texture of bark. Spoon the chocolate shavings evenly over the frosted cake, covering the top and sides, and pressing gently on the shavings to help them adhere.

12 Serve the cake

Using a large, sharp knife and a light sawing motion, cut the cake roll into 10–12 slices each 1–1¼ inches (2.5–3 cm) thick. Or, carefully place on a cake plate with a lid and refrigerate for up to 3 days; bring to room temperature before serving to soften the buttercream.

PASTRY CHEF'S TIP

To tighten a frosted cake roll for a more compact finish, place the rolled cake horizontally on the lower third of a clean sheet of waxed paper. Bring the far edge of the paper over the roll, overlapping it by 3 inches (7.5 cm). Position a ruler at a 45-degree angle, pushing against the cake and securing the 3-inch overhang. At the same time, firmly pull the paper edge closest to you to compact the cake slightly.

Serving ideas

Bûche de Noël, one of the most popular of all rolled cakes, looks difficult to make, but with practice, it soon becomes easy. Once you have assembled the cake, decorating it can be fun. Candied rosemary sprigs and flowers add seasonal color, while a dusting of confectioners' sugar imitates freshly fallen snow. Or, use white chocolate curls in place of the dark chocolate curls for a stunning contrast with the dark buttercream.

Candied cranberries and rosemary sprigs (top left)
To make candied cranberries, follow the recipe on page 30 for candied citrus zest, replacing the zest with cranberries. To make candied rosemary, follow the recipe on page 31 for sugared flowers, replacing the flowers with rosemary sprigs. (These are just decorative; you don't want to eat them.)

Confectioners' sugar "snow" (left)
Put confectioners' (icing) sugar in a fine-mesh sieve and lightly sift it over the cake.

White chocolate curls (above)
Follow the instructions on page 45 to make white chocolate curls. Sprinkle them over the cake in place of the dark chocolate curls.

Cake Roll Variations

Once you have made the Bûche de Noël on page 113, you can practice your newly acquired skills—baking, filling, and rolling a sheet cake and making buttercream—on the rolled cakes presented here. Among them are an old-fashioned jelly roll, a strawberry-and-cream-filled cake roll, and chocolate-covered pinwheel slices. You can use blueberries or raspberries in place of the strawberries, vary the flavor of the buttercream or whipped cream, or change the flavor of the syrup for many more variations. Each variation makes 10–12 servings, except the Pinwheel Cakes, which yields 8 individual cakes. For the best results, always roll a sheet cake while it is still warm.

Mocha Cake Roll

Chocolate and coffee, classic flavor partners, mingle in this cake roll.

Bake and cool 1 Chocolate Sponge Sheet Cake (page 87).

Next, make a coffee syrup: In a small saucepan, stir together ¼ cup (2 fl oz/ 60 ml) water and ¼ cup (2 oz/60 g) granulated sugar over low heat until the sugar dissolves and the mixture is hot. Stir in 1½ teaspoons instant coffee powder and let cool.

Make 1 batch Vanilla Buttercream (page 20), use only 1 teaspoon vanilla extract (essence) and add 2 tablespoons instant coffee powder dissolved in 1 tablespoon water. Make chocolate curls from a 4-oz (125-g) block semisweet (plain) chocolate and put in the freezer to firm.

When ready to assemble, brush the cake with 4 tablespoons (2 fl oz/60 ml) of the coffee syrup, then spread 2 cups (16 fl oz/500 ml) of the buttercream over the cake. Roll up the cake into an even cylinder. Transfer the roll, seam side down, to a platter. Brush the remaining syrup over the cake roll, then frost with the remaining buttercream.

Finally, scatter the chocolate curls over the roll. Cut into slices and serve.

Raspberry Jelly Roll

This cake requires no frosting, just a simple dusting of confectioners' sugar.

Bake and cool 1 Vanilla Sponge Sheet Cake (page 87).

Next, make a raspberry syrup: In a small saucepan, stir together ¼ cup (2 fl oz/ 60 ml) water and ¼ cup (2 oz/60 g) granulated sugar over low heat until the sugar dissolves and the mixture is hot. Stir in 2 tablespoons raspberry liqueur and let cool.

In another small saucepan, warm 1½ cups (12½ oz/390 g) seedless raspberry jam over low heat, stirring often, just until it melts.

When ready to assemble, brush the cake lightly with the raspberry syrup. Using an icing spatula, spread the warm jam evenly over the cake. Roll up the cake into an even cylinder. Transfer the roll, seam side down, to a platter.

Finally, put 1½ tablespoons confectioners' (icing) sugar in a fine-mesh sieve. Tap the sieve lightly to release a fine dusting of sugar over the top of the cake roll. Cut into slices and serve.

Chocolate-Berry Cake Roll

Chocolate and raspberry pair well in this colorful cake roll.

Bake and cool 1 Chocolate Sponge Sheet Cake (page 87).

Next, make a raspberry syrup: In a small saucepan, stir together ¼ cup (2 fl oz/ 60 ml) water and ¼ cup (2 oz/60 g) granulated sugar over low heat until the sugar dissolves and the mixture is hot. Stir in 2 tablespoons raspberry liqueur and let cool.

Make 1 batch Vanilla Buttercream (page 20), but use only 1 teaspoon vanilla extract (essence) and add 2 tablespoons raspberry liqueur.

When ready to assemble, brush the cake with ¼ cup (2 fl oz/60 ml) of the raspberry syrup, then spread 2 cups (16 fl oz/ 500 ml) of the raspberry buttercream evenly over the cake. Roll up the cake into an even cylinder. Transfer the roll, seam side down, to a platter. Brush the remaining syrup over the cake roll, then frost with the remaining buttercream.

Finally, scatter 1 cup (4 oz/125 g) raspberries over the cake roll. Cut into slices and serve.

Orange Cream Cake Roll

Orange flavor permeates every element of this cake: batter, syrup, and filling.

Bake and cool 1 Vanilla Sponge Sheet Cake (page 87), mixing in 1 teaspoon grated orange zest with the vanilla extract (essence).

Next, make an orange syrup: In a small saucepan, stir together ¼ cup (2 fl oz/ 60 ml) water and ¼ cup (2 oz/60 g) granulated sugar over low heat until the sugar dissolves and the mixture is hot. Stir in 2 tablespoons Cointreau and let cool.

Make 1 batch Citrus Curd (page 26) using oranges, and refrigerate to chill.

In a large bowl, using a mixer or balloon whisk, beat 2 cups (16 fl oz/500 ml) cold heavy (double) cream, ¼ cup (1 oz/30 g) confectioners' (icing) sugar, and 1 teaspoon vanilla extract until stiff peaks form. Using a rubber spatula, fold in 1 cup (8 fl oz/250 ml) of the orange curd (save the rest for another use). Turn the mixer on medium-high speed and beat the orange cream until soft peaks form and the mixture is firm enough to spread on the cake.

When ready to assemble, brush the cake with ¼ cup (2 fl oz/60 ml) of the orange syrup, then spread 2 cups (16 fl oz/500 ml) of the orange cream over the cake. Roll up the cake into an even cylinder. Transfer the roll, seam side down, to a platter. Brush the remaining 2 tablespoons cake syrup over the roll.

Finally, frost the cake roll with the remaining orange cream. Cut into slices and serve.

Strawberry Roulade

Strawberries and whipped cream fill this light-textured cake roll.

Bake and cool 1 Vanilla Sponge Sheet Cake (page 87).

Next, make an orange syrup: In a small saucepan, stir together ¼ cup (2 fl oz/ 60 ml) water and ¼ cup (2 oz/60 g) granulated sugar over low heat until the sugar dissolves and the mixture is hot. Stir in 2 tablespoons Grand Marnier and let cool.

Stem 1½ cups (6 oz/185 g) strawberries and chop into ¼-inch (6-mm) pieces. Toss them in a bowl with 1 tablespoon granulated sugar. Let stand for about 10 minutes, then drain through a fine-mesh sieve, discarding the juices.

In a large bowl, using a mixer or balloon whisk, beat 2 cups (16 fl oz/500 ml) cold heavy (double) cream, ¼ cup (1 oz/30 g) confectioners' (icing) sugar, and 1 teaspoon vanilla extract (essence) until stiff peaks form. Set aside 2½ cups (20 fl oz/ 625 ml) of the whipped cream. Using a rubber spatula, fold the berries into the remaining cream.

When ready to assemble, brush the cake with ¼ cup (2 fl oz/60 ml) of the orange syrup, then spread the berry-cream mixture over the cake. Roll up the cake into an even cylinder. Transfer the roll, seam side down, to a platter. Brush the remaining 2 tablespoons syrup over the cake roll, then frost with the reserved whipped cream.

Finally, stem, core, and halve lengthwise 12 strawberries. Arrange cut side down in a line along the base of each side of the cake roll. Cut into slices and serve.

Pinwheel Cakes

Here, a cake roll is divided into 8 small cakes, then covered in chocolate glaze.

Bake and cool 1 Chocolate Sponge Sheet Cake (page 87).

Next, make a coffee syrup: In a small saucepan, stir together ¼ cup (2 fl oz/ 60 ml) water and ¼ cup (2 oz/60 g) granulated sugar over low heat until the sugar dissolves and the mixture is hot. Stir in 1½ teaspoons instant coffee powder and let cool.

Make 1 batch Vanilla Buttercream (page 20). Next, make 1 batch Chocolate Glaze (page 128).

When ready to assemble, brush the cake lightly with the coffee syrup, then spread the buttercream over the cake. Roll up the cake into an even cylinder. Smooth any buttercream at the seam of the cake roll so that even circles form when the cake roll is cut.

Using a serrated knife and a light sawing motion, cut the roll crosswise into 8 slices each 1¾ inches (4.5 cm) thick. Place the slices, cut side up, on a wire rack. Slide a large sheet of waxed paper under the wire rack to catch drips. Pour about 2 tablespoons of the glaze over 1 slice and, using an icing spatula, smooth the glaze evenly over the top and sides. Add more glaze if necessary to cover the top and sides completely. Repeat to glaze all of the pinwheels. Let the pinwheels stand until the glaze is firm, then serve.

Vanilla Cheesecake

Cheesecakes make perfect party desserts. They are simple to mix, can be made several days in advance, and have a satiny, dense texture and a rich, creamy taste that nearly everyone likes. Here, the crunch of the simple crumb crust contrasts nicely with the smooth filling and creamy topping.

1 Preheat the oven and prepare the pan

Position a rack in the lower middle of the oven, so the cake will be evenly surrounded with heat, and preheat to 325°F (165°C). Place a small amount of butter on a piece of waxed paper and spread the butter evenly over the bottom and sides of a 9-inch (23-cm) springform pan. Cut a large piece of heavy-duty aluminum foil and wrap the outside of the pan with the foil. The cheesecake will bake in a water bath, and the foil makes the pan watertight. Have ready a roasting pan at least 2 inches (5 cm) deep and large enough to hold the foil-wrapped springform pan to use for the water bath.

2 Make and prebake the crumb crust

If using whole graham crackers, place them into a locking plastic bag. Using a rolling pin, crush them until they form fine, uniform crumbs. Pour the crumbs into a bowl. Or, if starting with crumbs, simply measure them and put them into the bowl. Add the melted butter and, using a large spoon, stir together until the crumbs are evenly moistened. Pour the crumb mixture into the prepared pan and, using your fingers, press it evenly onto the pan bottom. Bake the crust until it turns slightly darker, about 10 minutes. Transfer to a wire rack and let cool slightly. (Prebaking a crust before filling it and baking again prevents it from absorbing too much liquid from the filling, thus eliminating sogginess.) Leave the oven on.

3 Beat the eggs for the filling

Crack the eggs into a small bowl and check for shell bits. Make sure the eggs are at room temperature. Cold eggs can cause bits of the cream cheese to firm up, creating white specks that do not disappear during baking. (If they are not at room temperature, let them sit for about 45 minutes to warm.) Using a fork, beat vigorously until the yolks and whites are blended. Set aside. ›

Unsalted butter for preparing the pan

For the crust

6 graham crackers or 1 cup (3 oz/90 g) graham cracker crumbs

¼ cup (2 oz/60 g) unsalted butter, melted

For the filling

4 large eggs, at room temperature

2 lb (1 kg) cream cheese, at room temperature

1⅓ cups granulated sugar

2 teaspoons vanilla extract (essence)

3 tablespoons all-purpose (plain) flour

¼ cup (2 fl oz/60 ml) heavy (double) cream

½ cup (4 oz/125 g) sour cream

For the topping

1½ cups (12 oz/375 g) sour cream

¼ cup (2 oz/60 g) granulated sugar

1 teaspoon vanilla extract (essence)

MAKES ONE 9-INCH (23-CM) CHEESECAKE, OR 16 SERVINGS

4>>

4 Make the filling

In a large mixing bowl or the bowl of a stand mixer, combine the cream cheese, sugar, and vanilla extract. Fit the handheld mixer with the twin beaters or the stand mixer with the paddle attachment. Beat on low speed until the mixture is well blended, about 1 minute. Stop the mixer occasionally to scrape down the sides of the bowl. If using a handheld mixer, move the beaters around in the bowl to make sure every bit of the mixture is well beaten. Add the flour and beat on low speed just until incorporated, about 1 minute. Add half of the beaten eggs and beat just until fully blended with the batter. Add the remaining half of the beaten eggs and again beat just until fully blended. Add the heavy cream and sour cream and beat just until no white streaks are visible, about 1 minute. Set aside.

5 Make the topping

In a small bowl, combine the sour cream, sugar, and vanilla extract. Using a whisk, beat the mixture until well blended. Set aside.

6 Assemble the cheesecake and water bath

Pour the filling onto the prebaked crust, using a spatula to scrape every last bit from the bowl. Put the filled springform pan in the roasting pan and carefully slide the roasting pan onto the oven rack. Fill a heatproof pitcher with hot water and slowly pour the water into the roasting pan until it reaches 1 inch (2.5 cm) up the sides of the springform pan. This is known as a *water bath*. It promotes gentle, even, moist baking and helps to eliminate cracking in the finished cheesecake.

7 Bake the cheesecake

Bake undisturbed for 55 minutes. If the cake looks set, give the pan a gentle shake, being careful not to splash any water. If the top wobbles, set the timer for another 5 minutes. Repeat this process until the cheesecake is done. Tiny cracks along the edges are an indication that the cheesecake is ready (They disappear as the cake cools.) It will probably take no more than 1 hour and 5 minutes.

8 Add the topping

Using pot holders, carefully remove the cheesecake, still in its water bath, from the oven. Use a narrow-bladed icing spatula to spread the sour-cream topping gently and evenly over the top of the baked cheesecake. Return the cheesecake in the water bath to the oven and bake until the topping firms slightly, about 10 minutes.

MAKE-AHEAD TIP

If you are concerned about marring the top of your cheesecake when you cover it for chilling, invert a large plate over the top of the pan before wrapping in plastic wrap.

9 Let the cheesecake cool

Using pot holders, transfer the cheesecake in the water bath to a wire rack. Let the cheesecake cool for 1 hour, then lift the springform pan from the water bath. Remove the roasting pan and return the springform pan to the rack. Remove the foil wrapping from the pan and let the cake cool on the rack for 1 hour longer. The top should feel cool to the touch. Cover with plastic wrap and refrigerate the cake in the pan for at least 6 hours or up to overnight before serving.

10 Unmold the cheesecake and serve or store

About 45 minutes before you plan to serve it, remove the cheesecake from the refrigerator to let the flavors emerge. Remove the plastic wrap and discard. Run a thin knife along the inside edge of the pan to loosen the cake, keeping the knife pressed against the pan sides. Release the pan sides and lift off. Using the thin knife, loosen the crust from the pan bottom. Slip the removable bottom of a tart pan or 2 wide metal spatulas about three-fourths of the way under the cheesecake and slide it onto a serving plate. If serving right away, cut the cheesecake into slices (see opposite page). Or, wrap the uncut cheesecake with plastic wrap and store in the refrigerator for up to 5 days.

Cutting a dense cake

Cutting through a moist, dense cake can leave a lot of extra cake on your knife, making it messy and difficult to use. To keep slices neat and uniform and the knife blade clean, heat the blade of the knife before you cut each slice. Cut only the number of slices that you will be serving, to keep the balance of the cake from drying out. Once the slices are cut, use a triangular cake server to transfer the wedges to serving plates.

Heating the knife (top left)
Have ready a tall glass or pitcher filled with hot water and a long, sharp knife. Dip the knife in the water and let sit for a few seconds to warm the blade for cutting.

Wiping the knife clean (left)
Holding the sharp side of the knife away from you, wipe the blade dry with a paper towel.

Cutting even slices (above)
Using the hot knife, lightly score the topping to divide the cake into halves and then into quarters. Within each quarter, mark more slices to equal the number of servings you need. Dip the knife in the water and wipe clean before each cut is made.

Cheesecake Variations

All the techniques—making a crumb crust, creating a smooth filling, assembling a water bath, unmolding the finished cake—you have mastered in Vanilla Cheesecake (page 121) can now be applied to baking cheesecakes infused with other flavors. The simple addition of such ingredients as espresso, chocolate, or lemon gives this classic cake a new flavor profile, while most of the other ingredients remain the same. Cap off your next celebratory dinner with White Chocolate Cheesecake. Or, for a special fall dessert, make the Pumpkin Cheesecake. Remember, these cakes can all be made in advance. Each variation makes 16 servings.

Espresso Cheesecake

The addition of only a small amount of espresso powder imparts a robust coffee flavor to this cake.

Follow the recipe for Vanilla Cheesecake, dissolving 2 tablespoons instant espresso powder into the heavy (double) cream before adding it to the mixture.

Omit steps 5 and 8 for the sour cream topping, and proceed with the recipe to bake and serve the cheesecake.

PASTRY CHEF'S TIP

If you are worried about your cheesecake cracking, cover it loosely with paper towels while it is cooling in the roasting pan. Be sure that the towels don't touch the cake, and that they don't get wet from the water in the bottom of the pan.

Chocolate Cheesecake

Ganache gives this variation a deep flavor and an appealing dark brown color.

Follow the recipe for Vanilla Cheesecake. Before stirring in the sour cream in step 4, mix in 1 cup (8 fl oz/250 ml) Ganache (page 28), which has been cooled to a pourable consistency, just until it is incorporated.

Omit steps 5 and 8 for the sour cream topping, and proceed with the recipe to bake and serve the cheesecake.

White Chocolate Cheesecake

Adding white chocolate to Vanilla Cheesecake makes it even richer and enhances the cake's creamy color.

Follow the recipe for Vanilla Cheesecake. Before stirring in the sour cream in step 4, mix in 8 oz (250 g) melted white chocolate just until it incorporated.

Omit steps 5 and 8 for the sour cream topping, and proceed with the recipe to bake and serve the cheesecake.

Marble Cheesecake

Here, a marbleized pattern is made by swirling chocolate ganache into the cheesecake batter.

Follow the recipe for Vanilla Cheesecake. After making the filling in step 4, transfer ½ cup (4 fl oz/125 ml) to a small bowl and stir in ½ cup (4 fl oz/125 ml) Ganache (page 28), which has been cooled to a pourable consistency, until the batter is uniform in color.

Pour the vanilla filling into the prepared pan and, using a small spoon, drizzle the chocolate filling over the vanilla filling. Using the tip of a small knife, gently swirl the chocolate filling into the vanilla filling to create a marbleized pattern on the surface. Do not extend the tip too deeply into the filling or you may pierce the crumb crust.

Omit steps 5 and 8 for the sour cream topping, and proceed with the recipe to bake and serve the cheesecake.

PASTRY CHEF'S TIP

Using low-fat or nonfat cream cheese for making a cheescake will not only result in a less satisfying taste but also a drier texture. Full-fat cream cheese delivers more moisture because of its higher fat content.

Lemon Cheesecake

Adding fresh lemon juice and finely grated lemon zest cuts the richness of the cheesecake, making a refreshingly indulgent dessert.

Follow the recipe for Vanilla Cheesecake. Before stirring in the sour cream in step 4, add 3 tablespoons fresh lemon juice and 2 tablespoons grated lemon zest and mix just until incorporated.

Omit steps 5 and 8 for the sour cream topping, and proceed with the recipe to bake and serve the cheesecake.

Pumpkin Cheesecake

Cinnamon, ginger, and rum heighten the flavor of pumpkin in this cheesecake, perfect for the fall months.

Follow the recipe for Vanilla Cheesecake. After you have added the second half of the beaten eggs in step 4, add 1½ teaspoons ground cinnamon, 1 teaspoon ground ginger, and 2 tablespoons dark rum and mix just until incorporated. Omit the heavy (double) cream. Then, after mixing in the sour cream, mix in 1½ cups (12 oz/375 g) canned solid-pack pumpkin just until it is smoothly incorporated into the filling. The filling will be a golden orange.

Omit steps 5 and 8 for the sour cream topping, and bake the cheesecake in the water bath for 1 hour and 20 minutes (the pumpkin makes the filling more liquid, which increases the baking time.) Serve the cheesecake as directed.

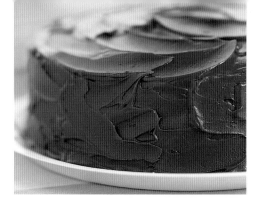

Classic Butter Cake (page 99), baked
as 2 round layers, and cooled

For the pastry cream

1½ cups (12 fl oz/375 ml) whole milk

4 large egg yolks

½ cup (4 oz/125 g) granulated sugar

2 tablespoons cornstarch (cornflour)

2 tablespoons unsalted butter, at room
temperature

1 teaspoon vanilla extract (essence)

For the chocolate glaze

8 oz (250 g) semisweet (plain) chocolate,
finely chopped (page 40)

½ cup (4 oz/125 g) unsalted butter, at room
temperature, cut into 8 equal pieces

1 tablespoon light corn syrup

MAKES ONE 9-INCH (23-CM) CAKE,
OR 12 SERVINGS

PASTRY CHEF'S TIP

*If you forget how many eggs you have
separated, you can weigh the yolks or
the whites. A single large yolk weighs
¾ ounce (20 g) and 1 large white
weighs 1¼ ounces (37 g). Divide the
total weight by the weight of a single
yolk or white to get the correct number.*

Boston Cream Pie

Despite its name, this Boston classic is nothing like a pie at all. It begins as a two-layered moist, tender-crumbed butter cake that has a well cut out of the bottom layer. The well is filled with thick, smooth pastry cream—an unexpected surprise. Then, the cake is topped off with a shiny chocolate glaze. Simply put, this cake is rich, and satisfying.

1 **Make and refrigerate the pastry cream**
While the cake is baking, make the pastry cream. In a heavy-bottomed saucepan over medium heat, warm the milk until tiny bubbles form along the pan edges. Remove from the heat. In a bowl, whisk together the egg yolks and sugar until blended. Add the cornstarch and whisk until smooth. Slowly pour the hot milk into the yolk mixture while whisking constantly. Return the mixture to the saucepan, place over medium heat, and stir constantly with a wooden spoon until the mixture thickens and just comes to a boil, 2–3 minutes. Pour the hot pastry cream through a fine-mesh sieve placed over a bowl. Add the butter and vanilla extract and stir slowly until the butter melts. Press a piece of plastic wrap directly onto the surface, poke a few holes in the plastic with a thin skewer or toothpick, and refrigerate until well chilled, about 2 hours.

2 **Make the chocolate glaze**
Pour water to a depth of 1½ inches (4 cm) into a saucepan, place over low heat, and bring to a bare simmer. Combine the chocolate, butter, and corn syrup in a heatproof bowl that fits securely into the pan without touching the water. Heat the mixture, stirring often with a heatproof silicone spatula, until melted and smooth. Let the glaze cool until it has thickened to a pourable consistency, about 20 minutes.

3 **Assemble the cake**
Place 1 cake, top side up, on a serving plate. Tuck narrow strips of waxed-paper about 1 inch (2.5 cm) under and all along the edges of the layer. Using a small knife and beginning ½ inch (12 mm) from the edge of the cake layer, mark a circle ½ inch deep in the cake layer. Use the knife to cut out the circle, creating an indentation 8 inches (20 cm) in diameter and ½ inch deep and leaving a ½-inch border. Eat or discard the removed cake. Using an offset icing spatula, spread the pastry cream in the indentation. Top with the second layer. Pour about half the glaze over the top of the cake and use a clean icing spatula to spread it evenly. Use the spatula to spread the remaining glaze onto the sides of the cake, turning the plate as needed to frost evenly.

4 **Serve or store the cake**
Remove the waxed paper strips. Using a large, sharp knife, cut the cake into wedges. Or, you can refrigerate the finished cake for 1 hour to firm the glaze, then cover it with plastic wrap and refrigerate for up to 2 days before serving; let stand at room temperature for 30 minutes before serving.

Individual Molten Chocolate Cakes

Deliberately underbaked, these chocolate cakes have centers reminiscent of warm fudge sauce and edges akin to a dense soufflé, a combination that makes them both irresistible and eye-catching. They are baked in ramekins and served in the same dishes for ease. A light sprinkle of confectioners' sugar dresses them up simply.

1 **Preheat the oven and prepare the ramekins**
Position a rack in the middle of the oven, and preheat to 350°F (180°C). Butter the bottom and sides of six ¾-cup (6–fl oz/180-ml) ovenproof ramekins, and put them on a rimmed baking sheet.

2 **Melt the chocolate with the butter**
If you are new to melting chocolate, turn to page 40. Combine the chocolate and butter in a large heatproof bowl and place over barely simmering water. Stir occasionally until smooth and all of the chocolate has melted. Remove the bowl from the pan and set aside to cool slightly.

3 **Make the batter**
Sift the flour through a fine-mesh sieve placed over a small bowl. Set aside. In the bowl of a stand mixer or a large mixing bowl, combine the eggs, sugar, and salt. Fit the stand mixer with the paddle attachment or a handheld mixer with the twin beaters. Beat the mixture on medium-high speed until it thickens and the color lightens slightly, about 4 minutes. Stop the mixer occasionally to scrape down the sides of the bowl. Reduce the speed to low, add the vanilla extract and dissolved coffee, and beat until combined. With the mixer running, add the flour 1 tablespoon at a time. Using a large rubber spatula, stir about one-third of the chocolate mixture into the egg mixture to lighten it. Scrape the remaining chocolate on top of the batter and, using the spatula, fold the mixtures together just until no streaks of the chocolate mixture are visible. For more details on the folding technique, turn to page 39.

4 **Bake the cakes**
Pour the batter into a 4-cup (32–fl oz/1-l) glass measuring cup, using the spatula to scrape out every last bit from the bowl. Pour about ½ cup (4 fl oz/125 ml) batter into each prepared ramekin. Bake until the edges look firm and dull on top and the center looks shiny and slightly wet, 16–18 minutes. You may see a few tiny holes on top. These cakes should be underbaked, so do not bake longer than 18 minutes.

5 **Serve the cakes**
Let the cakes cool in the ramekins on wire racks for 10 minutes. Put the confectioners' (icing) sugar in a fine-mesh sieve and sift an equal amount over the top of each cake. Using pot holders, transfer each ramekin to an individual serving plate. Serve right away.

Unsalted butter for preparing the ramekins

10 oz (315 g) semisweet (plain) chocolate, chopped

½ cup (4 oz/125 g) unsalted butter, cut into 8 equal pieces

¼ cup (1½ oz/45 g) all-purpose (plain) flour

4 large eggs

½ cup (4 oz/125 g) granulated sugar

¼ teaspoon salt

1 teaspoon vanilla extract (essence)

1 teaspoon instant coffee powder dissolved in 2 teaspoons hot water

1 tablespoon confectioners' (icing) sugar for dusting

MAKES 6 INDIVIDUAL CAKES

MAKE-AHEAD TIP
The batter can be poured into the ramekins up to 5 hours before serving and stored, wrapped, in the refrigerator. Let stand at room temperature for 20 minutes before baking.

Using Key Tools & Equipment

Having the right equipment on hand is indispensable to successful baking. If your pan is too large, your cake is sure to be disappointingly flat. Or, if your cake is soggy on the bottom, it's probably because you didn't cool it on a rack. The quality of the equipment is crucial as well. Buy the best mixer, pans, measuring cups, and other tools you can afford, and you'll be rewarded with decades of delicious homemade cakes.

Mixers

A high-quality stand mixer comes with three attachments—paddle, whip, and dough hook—for tackling a range of jobs with ease, and it leaves your hands free to add ingredients. Handheld mixers are a less expensive option and will work for any of the cake, filling, or frosting recipes in this book. Many come with a pair of wire beaters and a whip attachment.

Cake Pans

Choose layer pans made of heavy-gauge aluminum. Loaf pans can be metal or glass, and mini-muffin pans with a nonstick finish are preferred. For the recipes in this book, you'll need two 9-by-2-inch (23-by-5-cm) round layer pans, one 10-inch (25-cm) tube pan, one 9-inch (23-cm) springform pan, one 10-by-15-by-1-inch (25-by-38-by-2.5-cm) rimmed baking sheet, two 8½-by-4½ inch (21.5-by-11.5-inch) loaf pans, two 12-cup mini-muffin pans, and six ¾-cup (6–fl oz/180-ml) ovenproof ramekins. Always use the size pan called for in a recipe; a different-sized pan can adversely affect baking time and the final result.

Bowls

Select a nesting set of mixing bowls made of stainless steel, tempered glass, or ceramic. Stainless-steel or tempered glass bowls are the best choices because they can be heated safely. Aluminum bowls, which can react with acidic ingredients, or plastic bowls, which can retain odors or absorb fats, are less desirable. Copper bowls are ideal for beating egg whites. They should not, however, be used for mixtures that include acidic ingredients, such as lemon juice, as they will react with the acid, resulting in an off flavor.

You should always have all your ingredients ready before you begin to mix, so you need small bowls for holding them. You also need a heat-resistant bowl that fits snugly in the rim of a saucepan, for creating a double boiler.

Measuring Equipment

Two types of measuring cups are needed, one for dry ingredients and one for wet ingredients. Dry measuring cups usually come in sets of four graduated sizes, ¼ cup, ⅓ cup, ½ cup, and 1 cup. Sturdier stainless-steel cups are preferred over plastic ones. For greater accuracy, use a scale to measure dry ingredients.

Liquid measuring cups look like small pitchers, with horizontal markings that indicate fluid ounces, partial cups, and at least 1 cup (8 fl oz/250 ml). The same spoons are used for measuring both wet and dry ingredients.

Spoons & Spatulas for Stirring

Wood is a poor conductor of heat, so wooden spoons are handy for stove-top use. Metal spoons of various sizes are ideal for transferring chocolate shavings to cake tops, creating swirls in frosting, and drizzling a glaze. Rubber spatulas are used for scraping bowls clean, for folding lighter ingredients into heavier ones, and for general mixing. Silicone spatulas are heat-resistant, making them good for stove-top stirring.

Whisks

You'll need two types of wire whisks: a medium-sized utility whisk with fairly stiff, fairly coarse wires and a larger, rounder-headed balloon whisk with thinner wires and more of them. The first is used for vigorously stirring mixtures until smooth, while the latter is used for whipping cream or egg whites.

Knives, Graters & Peelers

Three basic knives are needed for making and serving cakes. A paring knife makes quick work of peeling and cutting fruit and removing the core of an apple or pear. A large chef's knife cuts most cakes into neat slices. A long serrated knife is the best choice for splitting cake layers horizontally, serving airy sponge cakes, and cutting chocolate into pieces.

A plastic or wooden cutting board cleans up easily with soap and water. Designate a cutting board for baking only, so that it stays free of odors from garlic, onion, or the like.

The handheld rasp, comes in two styles: one has small holes for finely grating citrus zest. A sturdy stainless-steel swivel-bladed vegetable peeler is handy for peeling fruit and shaving chocolate curls. A handheld reamer is helpful for extracting juice from citrus.

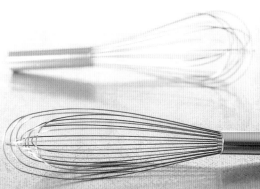
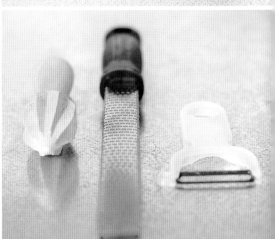

Sieves

Wire-mesh sieves are available in a variety of sizes, from small to large, with either fine or coarse mesh. Fine mesh works best for aerating ingredients such as flour, for getting the clumps out of confectioners' (icing) sugar, or for straining pastry cream. To accommodate varying amounts, it's handy to have an assortment of sizes, although a medium-sized sieve is a good all-purpose choice. Some sieves have a long handle and a metal hook that allows them to stay firmly balanced on the rim of a bowl.

Saucepans

Stainless-steel lined copper, or anodized aluminum saucepans are ideal. You'll want to have a 1-quart (1-l) saucepan for melting butter, a 2-quart (2-l) heavy-bottomed saucepan for making sugar syrups and for assembling a double boiler, and a 3- or 4-quart (3- or 4-l) heavy-bottomed saucepan for larger amounts of ingredients.

Thermometers

An instant-read thermometer, which consists of a long stem with a head that indicates the temperature, is handy for checking the temperature of water and of stove-top custards and curds. A mercury-type oven thermometer that hangs from or sits on the oven rack is indispensable for making sure your oven is accurate. Preheat the oven, check the temperature, and then adjust the control knob as needed if the actual temperature differs from the original setting. A candy thermometer registers very high temperatures and is good for measuring the stages of the cooked sugar syrups used in making buttercream (it can also come as a mercury bulb and column attached to a metal casing and a clip that slips over the pan side).

Cooling Racks

Cakes hot from the oven are nearly always cooled on sturdy wire racks that allow air to circulate and discourage condensation. Racks come in a variety of sizes—large, medium—and shapes—round, square, rectangular. They should be raised above the work surface by feet at least ½ inch (12 mm) high.

Brushes

Pastry brushes are used for applying syrups to cake layers and for washing down pan sides when making syrups. Small paint brushes are used to coat flower petals with egg whites. Look for

brushes with natural bristles that are solidly anchored in the handle. Wash well in soapy water after each use. Designate brushes for pastry purposes only, to avoid unwanted flavors.

Spatulas for Icing

Known as an icing spatula or palette knife, a thin metal spatula with a blade about 1 inch (2.5 cm) wide makes quick work of spreading and smoothing cake fillings and frostings and smoothing glazes. A small icing spatula with an offset blade—the blade is set at an angle to the handle—also works well.

A wider metal offset spatula is handy for smoothing the top of a batter, for lifting a cake layer onto a serving plate, and for applying frosting. You can also use a large icing spatula with blunt edges to frost a cake.

Pastry Bag and Tips

Choose a 16-inch (40-cm) pastry (piping) bag made of durable plastic-coated canvas. It will hold all the frosting you need to decorate a cake. Wash and rinse the bag thoroughly after each use and, if possible, dry on a sunny windowsill to prevent musty odors from developing. Disposable sturdy plastic pastry bags are another option. Have on hand a standard set of good-quality metal or plastic decorating tips—plain, fluted, and star—in several sizes. The white plastic coupler makes it easy to change tips without emptying the frosting out of the bag. Try to buy a standard set of tips that has a coupler included.

Miscellaneous Items

You'll need parchment (baking) paper for lining cake pans and baking sheets,

a ruler for measuring pans and cakes for cutting, and a timer to remind you to check beating and baking times. Thin skewers or toothpicks are ideal for checking if a cake is done. You'll also want to have thick pot holders to protect your hands from hot pans.

Serving Plates

Use large, flat plates, either round, square, or rectangular, depending on a cake's shape, for serving. Pedestal plates, with a fixed top are also attractive for serving layer cakes. A wide, metal triangular serving spatula eases serving individual slices. Dome-shaped cake covers (not pictured), which shield the cake without touching it, are ideal for storing freshly frosted cakes. Airtight tins or plastic containers (not pictured) are good for storing unfrosted cakes.

Glossary

ALMOND PASTE A finely ground mixture of almonds, sugar, glucose, and water, almond paste is used for adding flavor and texture to such cakes as Almond Pound Cake (page 55). It is available in cans or sealed plastic tubes that keep it fresh and moist. Be sure to purchase almond paste, rather than marzipan, which is sweeter.

APPLES Apples are an excellent way to add flavor and texture to a plain cake batter. Choose varieties that are good for baking, such as Granny Smith, Newton pippin, or Rome Beauty. Look for firm fruits with a good color and no soft spots.

BAKING POWDER A chemical leavener, baking powder reacts with liquids and heat to release carbon dioxide gas, which in turn causes a batter to rise as it bakes. Cornstarch is a typical component of baking powder, absorbing moisture to keep the powder dry until liquid is added. Store baking powder in an airtight container in a cool, dark place for up to six months.

BAKING SODA Also called bicarbonate of soda or sodium bicarbonate, baking soda is a chemical leavener that releases carbon dioxide gas only when it comes into contact with an acidic ingredient, such as sour cream, buttermilk, or citrus juice. Baking soda can be stored in an airtight container in a cool, dark place for up to six months.

BATTER A smooth, wet mixture that is thin enough to pour or spoon. Most cake batters consist of flour, eggs, butter or another fat, sugar, and a liquid, such as milk.

BEAT, TO To mix vigorously until a single ingredient, such as eggs, or a mixture, such as a cake batter, is smooth, well blended, and aerated. Beating is often accomplished with an electric mixer, although it can also be done by hand with a spoon or whisk.

BUTTER Unsalted butter is preferable to salted because it allows the baker more control over the flavoring of a cake. In addition, unsalted butter tends to be fresher because salt acts as a preservative, lengthening the shelf life of butter at the supermarket.

European-style butter, made from fermented cream, contains more butterfat and less water than regular butter, giving it a pure, rich buttery flavor. Store unsalted butter in the refrigerator for up to 1½ months or in the freezer for up to 6 months.

BUTTERCREAM A light, fluffy mixture of butter, sugar, and eggs used as a cake frosting or a filling. It can be flavored in several ways, including coffee, chocolate, and vanilla.

BUTTERMILK Traditionally, buttermilk is the liquid left behind when butter is churned from cream. Today, most buttermilk is a form of cultured low-fat or nonfat milk in which the sugars have turned to acids.

CARAMELIZE, TO To heat sugar until it melts and turns light to dark brown, developing more complex flavors. Sugar is considered caramelized when it registers between 320° and 350°F (160° and 180°C) on a candy thermometer. Adding caramelized sugar to fruits is key to such cakes as Pineapple-Upside Down Cake (page 67).

CHOCOLATE
Originally from Central America but now cultivated in other equatorial regions, chocolate is produced by roasting and crushing cacao beans to produce "nibs," or kernels. The nibs are then pressed into a paste known as chocolate liquor. To store chocolate, tightly wrap in aluminum foil and keep at cool room temperature. Dark chocolate will keep for up to 1 year, while milk chocolate and white chocolate should be used within 3 months.

Cocoa Powder When most of the cocoa butter is removed from chocolate liquor and the liquor is ground, unsweetened cocoa powder is the result. It is available in two types, regular and Dutch process. The latter is treated with an alkali solution, producing a milder flavor and darker color, and is preferred for the recipes in this book.

Dark Made from chocolate liquor sweetened with sugar and blended with additional cocoa butter. In general, European dark

chocolates are called bittersweet, while American dark chocolates are called semisweet (plain).

Milk Made from chocolate liquor to which both sugar and milk solids have been added, milk chocolate is sweeter than bittersweet or semisweet chocolate.

White Made from cocoa butter, milk solids, sugar, and flavorings. White chocolate contains no chocolate liqueur and therefore, is not a true chocolate.

COCONUT, SHREDDED Plastic bags or cans of shredded coconut are sold in the baking-supply aisles of supermarkets and smaller grocery stores. It is available in two forms, sweetened and unsweetened, with the latter more commonly stocked in natural-food stores.

COFFEE POWDER, INSTANT Made by heat drying freshly brewed coffee and reducing it to a powder, this versatile product is used for flavoring batters, frostings, and syrups.

COINTREAU An orange-flavored liqueur, Cointreau adds deep flavor to cake syrups. Other orange liqueurs, such as Triple Sec or Grand Marnier, may be substituted.

COPPER BOWL Copper bowls are ideal for beating egg whites because the copper chemically interacts with the albumin in the whites, which helps to stabilize them so that they are better able to hold air. When beating egg whites in a copper bowl, do not add cream of tartar, and transfer the whites to another bowl as soon as they are whipped. Copper bowls should not be used for mixtures that include acidic ingredients, such as lemon juice, as they will produce an off flavor.

CORE, TO To remove the central core, or seeds and/or stem, from a fruit such as an apple or strawberry.

CORNSTARCH Also called cornflour, cornstarch is a highly refined, silky powder ground from the endosperm of corn—the white heart of the kernel. It can be used as a neutral-flavored thickening agent in glazes and fillings such as pastry cream (page 128). Recipes that call for cornstarch require cooking to eliminate any starchy taste.

CORN SYRUP This syrup, made from cornstarch, is a common commercial sweetener that is also used in baking. Available in dark and light versions, it adds moisture to cakes.

COUPLER A small, two-piece plastic device consisting of a round grooved insert and a ring to tighten it, that is used in a pastry (piping) bag. The coupler makes it easy to change piping tips without changing pastry bags. It also prevents the contents of the bag from leaking out around the tip.

CREAM CHEESE A mild, tangy fresh cheese made from whole milk and extra cream that is often the primary ingredient in cheesecakes. Some bakers prefer "natural" cream cheese for its taste and because it does not contain stabilizers or additives present in most commercial brands.

CREAM, HEAVY Also known as heavy whipping cream, whipping cream, and double cream, heavy cream is high in milk fat and has a rich flavor. Do not substitute light cream or half-and-half (half cream) for the heavy cream called for in the recipes in this book. Avoid purchasing ultrapasteurized cream, which has been heated to extend its shelf life and does not whip as well.

CREAM OF TARTAR This powdery, white substance, technically known as potassium tartrate, is a by-product of wine making. It stabilizes and promotes volume when whipping egg whites and delivers greater loft and whiter, finer crumbs in cakes.

CREAMING A process in which fat, such as room-temperature butter, or fat plus another ingredient, such as butter and sugar, are beaten until soft and smooth. Creaming aerates the fat, which lightens the cake.

CRÈME DE CACAO A liqueur made from dark chocolate and a hint of vanilla. In cake making, it's used mostly for flavoring cake syrups and frostings.

CURD A thick, custardlike filling made from eggs, butter, and sugar, curd is often flavored with the juice and zest of citrus fruit, usually lemon or lime.

DOUBLE BOILER A set of two pans, one nested atop the other, with room for water to simmer in the bottom pan. Delicate foods, such as chocolate and custards, are placed in the top pan to heat gently, or to melt in the case of chocolate. The top pan should not touch the water beneath it, and usually the water is kept at a very gently simmer. A tight fit between the pans ensures that no steam can escape, which can cause melting chocolate to seize, or stiffen. You can create your own double boiler by placing a heatproof bowl or a slightly smaller saucepan over a larger one.

EGGS Eggs are sometimes used uncooked in meringues and other preparations. Although the incidence of salmonella or other bacteria in eggs is statistically extremely low, many cooks believe precautions must be taken. This risk is greatest to young children, elders, pregnant women, and anyone with a compromised immune system. If you have health and safety concerns, do not consume raw eggs. In some cases, pasteurized egg products can replace them. To store, leave eggs in their original carton and store in the refrigerator. Use them by the sell-by date stamped on the package.

ESPRESSO POWDER, INSTANT Similar to instant coffee powder, this powder can add the full flavor of espresso-roast coffee beans to cakes and cake syrups. Look for it in the coffee section of well-stocked food stores or Italian delicatessens.

EXTRACTS Concentrated flavorings made from plants, extracts, also called essences, are often used to flavor batters, frostings, and syrups. The most common extracts used in this book are vanilla, almond, and coconut. Pure vanilla extract is made by steeping vanilla beans, preferably Bourbon-Madagascar or Tahitian, in alcohol to extract their flavor, whereas pure almond extract is based on oil of bitter almond. Never use imitation flavorings, which can lend a chemical taste.

FIGS Soft, pear-shaped figs with their many tiny seeds are actually swollen flowers turned in on themselves. Among the best-known varieties are the small, dark

purple, sweet-tasting Mission or Black Mission and the gold-skinned Calimyrna. When dried, figs are even sweeter and delightfully chewy.

FLOUR The product that results from grinding grains, dried vegetables, or nuts into a fine powder. The two types of flour used in this book are both wheat flours. The first, all-purpose (plain) flour, is a blend of hard wheat, which has a high protein content, and soft wheat, which has a low protein content. Protein contributes to the development of gluten, which means that cakes made from all-purpose flour have a sturdier crumb. Cake flour, which is milled from soft wheat only, is more finely ground than all-purpose flour, has little protein, and yields a more delicate crumb. Store flours at room temperature in tightly covered containers for up to 6 months.

FLOWERS, EDIBLE Various edible fresh flowers may be candied for garnishing cakes. The best choices are small blossoms with simple petal configurations that can easily be brushed with egg white and coated with sugar. These include violets, pansies, small roses, and Peruvian lilies. Be sure to use only flowers that are grown for consumption and are free from pesticides.

FOLDING This simple but crucial technique is used to blend two mixtures (or ingredients) of different densities without losing volume or loft. It important to fold quickly and to stop folding once the mixtures are just blended, or they will deflate the batter.

FROSTING A thick, fluffy mixture, such as buttercream, used to coat the outside of a cake. The term is often used interchangeably with icing, although the latter is usually shinier and thinner. Frostings can also be used to fill cakes.

GANACHE A smooth mixture of melted chocolate and cream. While still barely warm, it is poured over cakes to form a smooth glaze. Cooled ganache can be whipped and used as a cake filling.

GLAZE Thinner than either a frosting or an icing, a glaze is poured, drizzled, or brushed on cakes. Many glazes harden once they are applied, becoming smooth and shiny and sometimes adding a bit of texture.

GLUTEN The weblike structure that forms in a batter due to the protein present in certain flours, including all-purpose (plain) flour and cake (soft-wheat) flour. Gluten helps to form the structure of a cake and can be controlled by the type of flour you use.

GRAHAM CRACKERS Whole-wheat (wholemeal) crackers that are sweetened with honey. In cake making, graham crackers are often crushed to make a crumb crust for cheesecakes.

GRAND MARNIER Grand Marnier is the grande dame of orange-flavored liqueurs, which also include Cointreau, Curaçao, and Triple Sec. Grand Marnier is made by flavoring brandy with bitter orange peel, vanilla, and spices. It is typically sipped over ice when not being used—always sparingly—in desserts and dessert sauces.

GRATE, TO To render a food into tiny particles, usually by rubbing it over the sharp, pointy rasps on a box grater-shredder. Typically done to help food, such as citrus zest, blend into a batter more quickly and easily.

HONEY The natural, sweet, syruplike substance produced by bees from flower nectar, honey subtly reflects the color, taste, and aroma of the blossoms from which it was made. Milder varieties, such as clover and orange blossom, are the best choices for most cake making.

ICING Used to coat and/or fill a cake, an icing is similar to a frosting, and the two terms are frequently used interchangeably. An icing is generally thinner and glossier.

KIRSCH A cherry-flavored colorless brandy, the best of which is made in Germany, France, and Switzerland, where the wild black cherry, native to the Rhine Valley, is used. In cake making, it is generally used for flavoring syrups and frostings.

LEMONS This small but versatile fruit was first cultivated in tropical regions of Asia and India before the Moors introduced it to Europe. Today, the most popular varieties

found in grocery stores are Eureka and Lisbon. The Meyer lemon, which can also be used, has a softer flesh as well as a sweeter flavor and a floral fragrance.

MACERATE To soak a food, usually fruit, in sugar and/or a flavorful liquid, such as liqueur, to draw out the juices, enhance its flavor, and sometimes soften its texture.

MANGOES First grown in India and now cultivated in other tropical regions, these fragrant, oval-shaped fruits have skin that ranges from green to pale yellow or orange with a light to deep yellow flesh. Choose fruits that give slightly to light pressure and are fragrant near the stem end.

MERINGUE Sweet, white, and fluffy, this delicate mixture is produced by beating together egg whites and sugar. A meringue can be soft, glossy, and smooth for covering cakes and is a necessary component for such frostings as Vanilla Buttercream (page 20).

MILK The rich flavor of whole milk comes from its emulsified fats, its distinctive white color derives from casein protein, and its faintly sweet flavor reveals the presence of lactose, a type of sugar found only in milk and its byproducts. Almost all milk sold today is homogenized, which means that it has been forced through tiny holes to break its fat globules into small particles that will remain suspended evenly throughout the liquid. If not homogenized, whole milk will have a layer of cream on top. Be sure to use whole milk in the recipes in this book that specify it. Low-fat or nonfat milk will not yield the desired rich results.

NUTS

Nuts provide richness, flavor, and crunch to many cakes. Most nuts have a hard shell, a protective coating developed by plants to shield their seeds from hungry animals. The high oil content of nuts means they turn rancid easily. Since freshness is crucial, always store them properly. Pack nuts in tightly capped jars or plastic containers or locking plastic bags and store in the refrigerator for up to 3 months or in the freezer for up to 6 months.

Almonds These oval nuts are found inside the pit of a dried fruit related to the peach.

Almonds are delicate and fragrant and have a smooth texture. They are sold unblanched, with their natural brown skins intact, and blanched, with the skins removed to reveal their light ivory color.

Hazelnuts Also known as filberts, grape-sized hazelnuts have hard shells that come to a point like an acorn, cream-colored flesh, and a sweet, rich, buttery flavor. Difficult to crack, they are usually sold already shelled.

Walnuts The furrowed, double-lobed nutmeat of the walnut has an assertive, rich flavor. The most common variety is the English walnut, also known as Persian walnut, which has a light brown shell that cracks easily. Black walnuts have a stronger flavor and extremely hard shells but are a challenge to find.

OILS For making most cakes, choose a bland-tasting oil such as canola or corn oil, which will add moisture without adding unwanted flavor. Store oils in airtight bottles away from heat and light.

PARCHMENT PAPER Treated to withstand the high heat of an oven, parchment paper is ideal for lining cake pans. Also known as baking paper, it resists moisture and grease and has a smooth surface that prevents cakes from sticking. Look for parchment paper in well-stocked markets and cookware shops.

PASTRY CREAM A basic custard that is used as a filling for cakes. The main ingredients are milk, eggs, sugar, flour or cornstarch (cornflour), and a flavoring, usually vanilla.

PEARS Like apples, pears can add a lot of flavor to plain cake batters. Choose varieties that are in season and good for baking, such as Bartlett (Williams'), Anjou, or Connie. Look for fruits free of blemishes, just beginning to soften, and with their stems still attached.

PINEAPPLE Its oval shape and rugged, scalelike texture inspired the Spanish to name the pineapple after a *piña*, or pinecone. Long cultivated in South America and the West Indies, the pineapple took Europe by storm after the explorers returned with samples of the fragrant, sweet, juicy fruit. The pineapple is now cultivated in hot regions from Hawaii to Malaysia. It ranks as one of the world's most popular tropical fruits and stars in the iconic Pineapple Upside-Down Cake (page 67). Fresh pineapples have deep green healthy leaves and give slightly to pressure.

PIPE, TO To make decorative effects on cakes by spooning frosting, whipped cream, or a similar mixture into the wide end of a pastry (piping) bag and then forcing, or piping, it out of the bag's narrow tip.

RUM, DARK Distilled from sugarcane juice or molasses, this Caribbean liquor comes in different colors, each stronger in flavor, from milk white or silver to golden, amber, dark, and Demerara, the darkest. Rum is used in this book as a flavoring for cake syrups.

SALT The most basic and ancient of seasonings. Varieties include table salt, sea salt, and kosher salt. Table salt usually contains added iodine along with additives that prevent it from caking so that it flows freely. Sea salt, by contrast, rarely has additives, and contains more minerals than table salt. It is available in coarse or fine grains that are shaped like hollow, flaky pyramids. Kosher salt has large, coarse flakes that are easy to handle and usually contains no additives or preservatives. Table salt was used to test the recipes in this book.

SIFT, TO To pass an ingredient such as sugar or flour through sieve or sifter to aerate it, give it a uniform consistency, and eliminate any large particles.

SOUR CREAM Cream to which a special bacterial culture has been added to produce lactic acid, which sours the cream. With its distinctive, clean tang and velvety texture, sour cream adds a luxuriant touch to baking recipes and is the basis for the topping in Vanilla Cheesecake (page 121).

SPICES
Essential oils are the source of flavor in spices, but they will dissipate over time, so replace your spices periodically. Purchase spices in small amounts from stores with high turnover and label them with the date of purchase. For the best flavor, use whole spices and grind them fresh. If stored in

tightly closed containers in a cool, dark place, ground spices will keep for about 6 months and whole spices for about 1 year.

Cinnamon The dark bark of a tree, the most commonly found variety is cassia cinnamon, which is a dark red-brown and has a strong, sweet taste. Cinnamon is available in stick form or ground.

Cloves Shaped like a small nail with a round head, the almost-black clove is the dried bud of a tropical evergreen tree. Cloves have a strong, sweet flavor with a peppery quality and are available whole or ground.

Ginger Fragrant and flavorful, this knobby rhizome, or underground stem adds a spicy-sweet flavor. It is available fresh, ground, and crystallized (candied in sugar syrup and then coated with granulated sugar).

Nutmeg The oval brown seed of a soft fruit, a nutmeg has a hard shell covered by a membrane that is removed, dried, and marketed as mace, another distinctive spice. Whole nutmeg keeps its warm, sweet flavor much longer than ground, and can be freshly grated as needed with a special nutmeg or other fine rasp grater.

Poppy seeds These tiny seeds add crunch and a slightly nutty flavor to foods. Be sure to use black poppy seeds, rather than brown seeds, for the recipes in this book.

SUGAR
Sugar used for baking comes in many forms and is most commonly processed from sugarcane or sugar beets. Keep sugars in tightly covered containers in a clean, dry place. They will last indefinitely.

Brown Rich in flavor, brown sugar is granulated sugar colored with molasses. It has a soft, moist texture and comes in two main types, mild-flavored light brown and strong-flavored dark brown.

Confectioners' Also called powdered or icing sugar, confectioners' sugar is granulated sugar that has been crushed to a powder and mixed with a little cornstarch (cornflour) to prevent caking.

Granulated The most common sugar in cake making, granulated white sugar has been extracted from sugarcane or sugar beets and

refined by boiling, centrifuging, and straining. For baking recipes, buy only sugar that is specifically labeled cane sugar; beet sugar can have an unpredictable effect.

Superfine When finely ground, granulated sugar becomes superfine sugar, also known as caster sugar. Because it dissolves rapidly, it is preferred for delicate mixtures. To make your own, process granulated sugar in a food processor until it forms fine granules.

TUBE PAN Any cake pan with a central tube, a feature that helps the center of a cake rise and bake evenly. Popular styles are the angel food cake pan, with a tall central tube and removable bottom, and the Bundt pan, with fluted sides and a rounded base.

VINEGAR, CIDER Made from apples, cider vinegar can be found in many traditional American recipes and is used for its flavor and also as a preservative.

WAXED PAPER Tissue-thin paper that has been coated on both sides with wax, making it moisture-resistant but not heat-resistant. Use waxed paper to sift ingredients onto or for lining cake plates before frosting a cake.

WHIPPING The process of beating a food, such as heavy (double) cream or egg whites, to increase its volume by incorporating air into it. Whipped ingredients are sometimes used to lighten the texture of heavier mixtures, such as folding whipped egg whites into a cake batter to facilitate rising.

ZEST The outer colored portion of the citrus peel, which is rich in flavorful oils. You can remove zest with a rasp grater or on the finest rasps on a box grater-shredder. Only remove the colored portion and not the bitter white pith underneath When choosing citrus for zesting, look for organic fruit, since pesticides concentrate in the peels.

Index

ƒP

FREE PRESS

A Division of Simon & Schuster, Inc.
1230 Avenue of the Americas
New York, NY 10020

WILLIAMS-SONOMA

Founder & Vice-Chairman Chuck Williams

WELDON OWEN INC.

Chief Executive Officer John Owen
President and Chief Operating Officer Terry Newell
Chief Financial Officer Christine E. Munson
Vice President International Sales Stuart Laurence
Creative Director Gaye Allen
Publisher Hannah Rahill
Senior Editor Jennifer Newens
Associate Editor Donita Boles
Editorial Assistant Juli Vendzules
Art Director Kyrie Forbes
Designers Marisa Kwek and Adrienne Aquino
Production Director Chris Hemesath
Color Manager Teri Bell
Production and Reprint Coordinator Todd Rechner
Food Stylist Alison Attenborough
Prop Stylist Leigh Nöe
Assistant Food Stylist Colin Flynn
Assistant Food Stylist and Hand Model Brittany Williams
Photographer's Assistant Mark Jordan

PHOTO CREDITS

Bill Bettencourt, all photography, except the following:
Mark Thomas: Pages 35–36, 37 (egg whites sequence), 38 (top right)
49 (second from right, right), 50 (right), 51 (second from left).

THE MASTERING SERIES

Conceived and produced by Weldon Owen Inc.
814 Montgomery Street, San Francisco, CA 94133
Telephone: 415 291 0100 Fax: 415 291 8841

In collaboration with Williams-Sonoma, Inc.
3250 Van Ness Avenue, San Francisco, CA 94109

A WELDON OWEN PRODUCTION
Copyright © 2005 by Weldon Owen Inc. and Williams-Sonoma Inc.

All rights reserved, including the right of reproduction in whole or in part
in any form.

FREE PRESS and colophon are registered trademarks of Simon & Schuster, Inc.

For information regarding special discounts for bulk purchases,
please contact Simon & Schuster Special Sales at 1 800 456 6798 or
business@simonandschuster.com

Set in ITC Berkeley and FF The Sans.

Color separations by Embassy Graphics.
Printed and bound in China by SNP Leefung Printers Limited.

First printed in 2005.

10 9 8 7 6 5 4 3 2

Library of Congress Cataloging-in-Publication data is available.

ISBN–13: 978-0-7432-6739-7
ISBN–10: 0-7432-6739-7

ACKNOWLEDGMENTS

Weldon Owen wishes to thank the following people for their
generous support in producing this book: Desne Ahlers,
Ken DellaPenta, Cris Eng, Emily Jahn, Linda Jahn, Ashley Johnson,
Karen Kemp, Renée Myers, Stephanie Munson, Aurora Noel,
Cynthia Scheer, Sharon Silva, Kate Washington, and Melinda Wright.

A NOTE ON WEIGHTS AND MEASURES

All recipes include customary U.S. and metric measurements. Metric conversions are based on
a standard developed for these books and have been rounded off. Actual weights may vary.